Cutting Edge Consultants

Other Books by Lawrence W. Tuller

Financing the Small Business

Recession-Proof Your Business

Going Global: New Opportunities for Growing Companies to Compete in World Markets

Tap the Hidden Wealth in Your Business

When the Bank Says No!: Creative Financing for Closely Held Companies

The Battle-Weary Executive: A Blueprint for New Beginnings

Buying In: A Guide to Acquiring a Business or Professional Practice

Getting Out: A Step-By-Step Guide to Selling a Business or Professional Practice

The McGraw-Hill Handbook of Global Trade and Investment Financing

Cutting Edge Consultants

Succeeding in Today's Explosive Markets

Lawrence W. Tuller

PRENTICE HALL
Englewood Cliffs, New Jersey 07632

Prentice-Hall International (UK) Limited, *London*
Prentice-Hall of Australia Pty. Limited, *Sydney*
Prentice-Hall Canada, Inc., *Toronto*
Prentice-Hall Hispanoamericana, S.A., *Mexico*
Prentice-Hall of India Private Limited, *New Dehli*
Prentice-Hall of Japan, Inc., *Tokyo*
Simon & Schuster Asia Pte. Ltd., *Singapore*
Editora Prentice-Hall do Brasil, Ltda., *Rio de Janeiro*

10 9 8 7 6 5 4 3 2 1

This publication is designed to provide accurate and authoritative information in regard to the subject matter covered. It is sold with the understanding that the publisher is not engaged in rendering legal, accounting, or other professional service. If
legal advice or other expert assistance is required, the services of a competent professional person should be sought.
*...From the Declaration of Principles jointly adopted by a Committee of the Ameri-
can Bar Association and a Committee of Publishers and Associations.*

Library of Congress Cataloging-in-Publication Data

Tuller, Lawrence W.
    Cutting edge consultants : succeeding in today's explosive markets /
Lawrence W. Tuller.
        p.   cm.
    Includes index.
    ISBN 0-13-194598-X
    1. Business consultants. I. Title.
HD69.C6T85   1992
001'.068—dc20   91-42057
                                                                 CIP

ISBN 0-13-194598-x

PRENTICE HALL
Professional Publishing
Englewood Cliffs, NJ 07632
Simon & Schuster, A Paramount Communications Company

Printed in the United States of America

Acknowledgments

Of all the consultants I have known and worked with over the years, no one deserves more credit for the content of this book than Ernest Perreault and Roman Fedirka. Without Ernest's guidance and patience I never would have succeeded in the international marketplace. Without Roman's enthusiasm for sharing his government contracting knowledge I would have said goodbye to Uncle Sam after the first DCAS battle. And of course, a special credit to my writing mentor, Mike Snell.

To Susan, Charles, and Maggie,
and especially to Barbara,
for seeing me through.

Preface

In recent years many long-term consultants have complained about the decrease in their client base. Consulting organizations, newsletters, and periodicals bemoan the maturity of the consulting profession (or industry as I prefer to call it) and warn of further deterioration. Yet the number of ex-executives, college graduates, and university instructors entering the field seems to multiply each year. Many fail: but many more make it.

How can it be that traditional consulting firms are losing business while newcomers are succeeding? Could it be that old-timers have grown soft, inflexible, secure in the belief that their markets of yesteryear remain inviolate? That the increasing numbers of consultants merely share the same markets, leaving lesser shares of the same pie for everyone? It might appear that way.

To me, however, these excuses beg the issue. Certainly the consulting industry is undergoing traumatic changes, as are most other industries. Obviously, economic downturns hurt consulting firms as much as any other business. Why shouldn't consultants feel the brush of austerity when times are tough? We certainly ride the wave of good fortune during economic booms.

But changes in the consulting industry go far beyond normal economic swings. Our markets, the clients that pay for our advice, are undergoing a revolutionary metamorphosis. To keep up we must leap aboard and adapt to changing times along with them. The alternative is to continue sulking in our plush offices, hoping for a miracle.

We must suppress our desire to call ourselves professionals as a means of elevating our status above the mundane business world.

We must roll up our sleeves and identify new, growth markets. We must learn new skills that these markets demand.

We must reassess our growth objectives along the same lines that we advise our clients.

We must return to business basics. We must research changing market demands, restructure our organizations and knowledge bases to service these demands, invest in the right tools to do the job, and not be fearful of growing, changing, and adapting along with our clients.

Above all, we must change the way we view the business arena. Good old laissez-faire days of free market economies (or semi-free) are over. A whole new paradigm of company ownership, controls, relationships, and values has taken over our clients, and we must learn to deal with it.

Technology refuses to allow us the luxury of ignorance. The upsurge of federal, state, and local government interference in private enterprise forces new approaches to dealing with these interlopers. Cross-border markets, financing, and resource allocation demands that we take a global view of our surroundings and adopt global rules for soliciting and servicing clients.

After twenty-five years in private industry and fourteen years in management consulting I refuse to acknowledge that consultants are unable to continue to lead the pack with new management techniques and state-of-the-art skills. Unwilling? Perhaps. Unable? Never.

In an effort to boost the morale of several old-line management consultants and to stimulate the enthusiasm of friends recently entering the business, I embarked on a mission to ascertain what, if any, future there might be for remaining in the consulting business.

Although certainly not scientifically conducted, this research reinforced my earlier suspicions. All doubts about the future of management consulting were removed. Enormous opportunities do indeed await those with vision. Rather than fading from sight, the consulting industry is on the threshold of a new generation of challenges.

I like to think that the consultants who will prosper over the next decade are dynamic, adventurous explorers, ready, willing, and able to meet the new challenges we are just beginning to recognize. These cutting-edge consultants will lead clients through the maze of new technologies, management techniques, financing options, and market opportunities to the global economy of the 21st century.

The one constant in each of the booming consulting markets examined in this book is the underlying necessity to view business opportunities through global glasses, to adopt a global mindset that carries this philosophy to client offices. Whether you specialize in government contracting or strategic planning; employee motivation techniques or solutions for troubled companies; small business start-ups or international finance; client markets, capital, resources, and competition take on a global hue. To exploit the global arena is to prosper; to ignore it leads to dead ends. Godspeed!

Lawrence W. Tuller

Berwyn, Pennsylvania

Contents

Chapter 3 □ ORGANIZING AND GETTING UP TO SPEED 43

Chapter 4 □ GETTING AND KEEPING CLIENTS 65

Chapter 5 □ PROJECT-ORIENTED MARKETS 85

Chapter 6 ☐ GENERAL MANAGEMENT MARKETS   105

Chapter 7 ☐ INTERNATIONAL CONSULTING MARKETS   127

Chapter 8 ☐ INTERNATIONAL FINANCING, COUNTERTRADE, AND ADMINISTRATION MARKETS   151

Chapter 9 ☐ TROUBLED COMPANY MARKET   177

Chapter 10 ☐ SMALL BUSINESS MARKET   199

Chapter 11 ☐ GOVERNMENT CONTRACTING MARKET   221

Chapter 12 ☐ THE FUTURE OF CONSULTING IN A CHANGING WORLD 241

1 *Winds of Change*

SOLUTION-PEDDLERS LOSE THEIR CHARM

Management consultants did well out of the last recession. This time they have been hit as hard as their clients. Worse, their fortunes may not recover when the economy revives.—*The Economist* February 9, 1991

Business consultants have been selling their recommendations for as long as private enterprise has existed. As long as companies continue to pay for "expert" advice, consultants stand ready to oblige. And just like any other industry, consulting has its economic cycles.

Consultants benefit from boom times along with everyone else. The industry newsletter *Consultants News* estimated a management consulting market of $3 billion in 1980. In 1990 this estimate rose to $22 billion! Consultants also suffer when times get tough. Most of the Big-6 accounting firms are laying off consulting staff by the hundreds. Peat Marwick asked 300 partners to take a walk. Ernst & Young has knocked down its overseas staff, especially in Great Britain. Even Arthur Andersen, sporting the world's largest consulting group—Andersen Consulting—is cutting costs to meet lower market demand.

Other large firms are trying to compensate by starting their own groups to concentrate on growing market niches or by merging with firms already rich in specialized talents. Booz, Allen & Hamilton started its Information Technology Group in the 1980s. McKinsey & Co. acquired a computer specialist firm. Pugh-Roberts of Cambridge, Massachusetts was snapped up by PA Consulting Group of Great Britain. The huge French firm Sogeti gobbled up United Research specializing in management change, the MAC Group formed by 400 academics to perform strategic consulting work, and the French firm Gamma International specializing in information technology.

Few would argue that the consulting business is currently in the throes of mammoth change. The industry structure that emerges from this worldwide reshuffling will be radically different from the consulting world of the past. Those consultants with the foresight and ability to redirect their organizations, skills, and marketing efforts will survive. Those glued to traditional consulting courses will surely continue down the long road to oblivion.

WHERE WE HAVE BEEN

Traditionally, mid-size and large consulting firms structure their organizations as a typical corporate bureaucracy: new recruits (juniors) do the on-site work, seniors supervise juniors, managers supervise seniors, and partners supervise managers. Client personnel work closely with juniors to compile and analyze company data. Seniors appear on the site to review the work of juniors. Then everyone retires to the consulting office and the manager reviews the same analyses and data.

In some firms, managers actually make recommendations based on this data. The analyses and recommendations then proceed to a partner, who does another review and either agrees with the manager's recommendations or makes additions or deletions. About this time, the partner returns to the client's office and reviews the firm's recommendations with the client. A report gets written and issued. Fees are billed and collected. That's the last the client sees of the consultants. The engagement is complete.

Each consultant level has an hourly billing range. The client pays for hours accumulated by each participant in the engagement at the individual's appropriate rate. All too frequently, a client spends thousands of dollars for a report filled with theoretical recommendations, many of which are totally impractical to implement. The client eventually forgets about the consultant and continues operating in the old way. Nothing has been accomplished except to line the consultant's pockets. And of course, the consulting firm does not get a repeat engagement.

A traditional organization structure constitutes only one of the maladies of the consulting business. The qualifications of consulting personnel is a second. Larger firms recruit young MBAs hot off the graduate school press, eager to demonstrate that they have learned the right way to manage a business. Their consulting supervisors expect great things from them. When confronted with actual operating problems in the field, however, these eager young people have only academic theory to draw upon, limiting their ability to offer practical solutions.

Eventually they work their way up the consulting ladder. The chosen few make partner. After years in the consulting business, these professional experts still have only their consulting observations to draw upon. Few, if any, ever get the opportunity for line, decision-making responsibility in a manufacturing, distribution, service, or retail environment.

On the flip side, business executives by the thousands, terminated for cost-cutting or other reasons, opt to try their hand at management consulting. Why not? Anyone can become a consultant without getting a license or passing an examination. All it takes is a telephone and letterhead. These consultants sell themselves as experts. In fact, their practical experience is often limited to a narrow range of activities that seldom applies directly to a client's problem areas. They perform the engagement, write a report filled with superfluous recommendations, collect their fee, and walk away. The client is no better off than if it had hired a large firm.

Even more troubling than cumbersome organizations and limited, outmoded skills are archaic marketing philosophies that leave consultants wondering where the next job will come from. A typical approach, popular in the consulting business for years, was expressed to me last year by an associate in Baltimore. "The whole trick in successful marketing is to identify what the client needs and then get out and sell it to him."

Drawing on years of experience in the business community, many of us believe we are experts in everything. Whatever the client's problem may be, we can solve it. Whether a client needs us for recruiting management personnel, developing a strategic plan, installing a computer system, locating new sources of funds, performing market research, analyzing pension benefits, or recommending cost-cutting programs, we can do it all. Tell us what problem needs solving; we'll sell you advice to do the job.

What many of us fail to recognize is that we are not capable of doing everything for everybody. We can't be all things to all people. We must specialize in market niches, develop definitive skills to serve these niches, concentrate only in those areas where we really are, or can become, expert.

WHERE WE ARE GOING

A new generation of better-informed owners and managers no longer accepts consulting mediocrity at high prices. They refuse to accept simple-minded solutions to complex issues. The days of gathering data, writing a report, and walking away are long gone. Clients want sophisticated answers to complicated problems. They want help implementing our recommendations. They want long-term gains, not quick fixes. They want solutions, not just advice. And more than anything else, clients want a sustaining relationship with a consultant who is qualified to give definitive and workable answers to specific operating questions.

As we all know, business consultants serve only two purposes: to solve problems with technical expertise or to solve problems with proven management techniques, neither of which is resident in client personnel. In both cases, the accent is on solving a client's problems. If clients didn't have problems that they couldn't handle themselves, they wouldn't need us. Client companies have the same characteristics as sick people. Sick people go to physicians for a cure. Sick companies go to management consultants for a cure.

As personal computers transform the shape and distribution of information, as management techniques evolve faster and more efficient means of producing and transporting products, and as money, customers, materials, and labor become truly globalized, the types of business problems also change. As client problems change so must consultants.

Five radical changes are occurring in the business community that consultants must deal with to ensure future success:

1. The onslaught of global competition. Companies of all sizes are rapidly learning that to remain competitive in their customary markets and to open new markets, they must incorporate global value-added production and marketing in their strategic plans. They must create products through which they can achieve the greatest cost and quality advantages in material sourcing and labor skills. They must raise capital in financial markets that offer the best terms and lowest cost. They must sell products to customers who will pay the highest price for the greatest volume of goods.

Giant competitors have sourced and sold globally for years. Now it's time for smaller and mid-size companies to join the parade.

2. The age of market specialization. The days of selling all things to all people are over. The medical profession learned years ago that keeping up with modern technology required concentrated specialties. Business firms such as Sears, Braniff Airlines, and the automobile manufacturers have now learned the same lesson. New technologies and sophisticated customers force manufacturing, distribution, retail, and service firms to concentrate rather than broaden their product lines.

3. Upheaval in the world financial system. The age of easy credit has led to the downfall of more than 200 American banks every year since 1987. Financial mismanagement and fraud resulted in the S & L debacle. Without radical changes in federal regulations the FDIC will be bankrupt before this year ends. Federal, state, and local governments face stringent restructuring to cope with unmanageable debt loans. Banks in Japan, the European Community, Eastern Europe, and Africa face imminent collapse. Middle Eastern banks have already lost significant reserves. The entire world financial system is in a state of flux with massive changes in cross-border financing on the horizon.

4. A revolution in social consciousness. Across the global spectrum demands for equality, social care, and freedom echo through the halls of governments and corporations. Usurpation of labor and abdication of employer responsibility have led to massive social reforms in government resource allocation and corporate policies.

Continued shifts toward environmentally safe products, guaranteed health care, and community development, are opening new doors and creating new problems for governments and private enterprise alike. Across America, and elsewhere to a lesser degree, disenchantment with corporate power games is driving individuals to seek their fortunes in entrepreneurial pursuits.

5. The "Star Wars" technology revolution. Advances in medicine, communications, and transport technologies heretofore relegated to comic books are opening enormous competitive advantages. They also create massive organizational, financial, and management problems. Ethical questions revolving around genetic engineering, environmental usurpation, and weapons of mass destruction confront social and corporate planners. Alternative energy sources obsoleting oil as a primary fuel portend huge changes in organization structure, product development, and the social impact of a vast array of products and industries. Materials technology will soon supersede ferrous and non-ferrous metals, forcing radical upheaval in industrial complexes and construction methodology.

NEW MARKET TRENDS

Two major trends are evolving from these macro-shifts: a broadening of management and technical expertise to deal with intensified competition, regulations, and social responsibilities; and a brain-drain out of business-oriented careers into science, social, governmental, and entrepreneurial fields. Both trends create an enormous need and market demand for specialists to assist businesses in coping with a changing world. What better source of expertise than management consultants? Where else can the world's managers turn for specific solutions to complex, ever-changing problems?

In turn, however, management consultants must be prepared. To survive the next decade, consultants will have to identify the range of new problems encountered by business clients. These, then, will become the new market niches that must be addressed. And consultants must develop new or updated skills to deal with them.

Some of these sizzling new markets require technical expertise: computer science, health care and rehabilitation, materials movement technology, chemical and biological analysis, and tax and estate planning, for example. Other red-hot markets demand state-of-the-art management skills, such as financial forecasting, international negotiating, material procurement and production scheduling, employee motivation methods, global finance sourcing, government contract procurement and management, and market and customer analysis.

To survive and prosper in the years ahead, management consultants must become cutting-edge consultants, conversant with the latest technologies and management techniques. They must not be afraid to experiment. They must not be leery of new methodologies and procedures. They must throw off the shackles of their traditional market niches, reorganize their firms, learn new skills, and carve out market niches that meet their specialized expertise. Cutting-edge consultants must set the pace for the management technology of the next century. To follow is to lose; to lead can only bring success.

Developing a cutting-edge consulting business requires a three-pronged approach:

1. Concentrate on the personal touch.
2. Sell specific, immediate help.
3. Structure solutions that bring long-term gains.

THE PERSONAL TOUCH

"Long-term relationships" with clients, "turning theory into reality," "making ideas work," and a variety of other slogans express the realization at many of the largest consulting firms that their engagements must entail concrete help leading to a client's long-term betterment rather than merely platitude-laden advice. But paying lip-service to the idea of relationship consulting and actually practicing it are two different conditions.

Few would argue that the most rewarding and long-lasting client engagements evolve from the personal relationships built up between a client's owner or manager and consultant. We all recognize how important the personal touch is to developing such a relationship. Yet, in the heat of battle, it's too easy to turn the leg work over to an employee or manager and reserve our effort for wrapping up the engagement. This may have worked in the past; it certainly will not in the future.

Consultants must be constantly aware of the nuances and perceptions that emanate during an engagement. In many cases, the client has turned over proprietary information, shared private wish lists, expressed long-secret hopes and fears to the consultant. Client personnel share themselves because they believe in the integrity and the loyalty of the consultant. Such a belief can only evolve by constant nurturing over a period of time, as client personnel and consultant get to know each other well and build a platform of mutual trust.

Trust cannot evolve without your concerted effort to make it happen. Nor can it occur in short engagements. Consultants must earn and then nurture a client's trust over an extended period. Time and again the personal touch leads to long-term relationships. And these relationships net higher fees, more satisfied clients, and stronger references for new clients.

At the peak of my consulting practice I was asked to help a client develop a strategic plan. Up to my ears in work, I really didn't have time to take on another assignment. Nevertheless I accepted the engagement.

This manufacturing client had suffered through a severe cash crunch two years earlier. My assignment at that earlier date was to help the owner turn his company around and untie some very knotty conflicts with his bank. It took nine months, but in the end we managed to resolve key issues, the client's business started picking up, and I located a new bank willing to extend additional credit.

The engagement required my full efforts for seven of the nine months. I put all other business on hold. A consulting associate warned me that this would hurt my business in the long run, that you can't work at production and market new clients at the same time. Nevertheless, I felt obligated to see this client through. With financial difficulties put to rest, I helped the client develop a strategic growth plan for the next ten years.

A write-up in the local newspaper describing how the owner had turned his company around brought direct solicitations from Arthur Andersen and a local consulting firm. The entrepreneur wrote both firms a letter with the closing sentences: "Larry Tuller has worked with me for 18 months. Without his direct help and personal concern

I wouldn't be in business today. I wouldn't dream of changing consultants now."

Management consulting has always been and will probably continue to be a personal service business. Without a close working relationship, consultants merely waste clients' money. Problem-solving advice is not enough. Consultants must also stand ready to help with the implementation of their recommendations.

Implementing changes in technical or operating practices requires a thorough grasp of the client's business, including all the nuances and relationships existing within the company. This cannot be obtained without becoming personally involved in the engagement. The personal touch is no longer optional; it has become mandatory.

THE URGENCY OF TODAY

During the easy credit, rapid growth era of the past decade, clients could afford to seek general consulting advice for long-term objectives. It looked good to board members, and to the investing public, for the company to garner consulting recommendations covering such diverse, long-range goals as developing a research and development program, expanding production facilities through merger or acquisitions, investigating alternate courses in government relations, and preparing long-range plans carefully bound with gold-embossed lettering. All were valid goals, but none were geared to solving today's problems today. Instead, they looked through rose-colored glasses at what "might be" feasible in the future—at a significant cost to clients.

The dreaming days are gone. In the new economy, clients need, and demand, answers to today's problems today. This does not mean that solutions must all be geared to short-term thinking. On the contrary, clients cannot afford to pay consulting fees for solutions that work today but will become obsolete tomorrow. The trick is to provide solutions to today's problems that will have long-range client benefits.

As an example, consider the case of an engagement I took to locate new sources for refinancing a burdensome debt structure. The client needed help now, but I had to be certain that the refinancing would be structured to meet the client's long-term objectives.

Through a personal banking connection I located a small venture capital fund that took out the bank debt in exchange for a 20 percent equity interest. In less than four years, with the expertise of the venture fund, my client went public with its first stock offering.

Regardless of the assignment, cutting-edge consultants should be acutely aware of a client's need for immediate action. A call to implement a personal computer network system doesn't mean you can wait three months to get it up and running. The client needs it now or you would not have been called. A similar situation exists in recruiting management personnel. If a client had several months to fill a slot it probably wouldn't need your help since the job could be done in-house. Calling on a consultant means that the client needs the job done now, not tomorrow.

This sense of urgency to find and implement solutions quickly and efficiently makes the difference between successful consultants and those still languishing in the dust. A reputation as a problem-solver with the ability to diagnose the problem and implement a solution in short order gets more new clients than any advertising could ever accomplish. Time and again, clients have told me that my reputation for doing what I say I'll do, when I say I'll do it, brought them to my door.

THE BENEFITS OF TOMORROW

Cutting-edge consultants must be extremely careful not to over-emphasize short-term solutions leading to the characteristic "quick-fix." Clients might appreciate and breathe a sigh of relief that one less problem needs attention, but "quick-fixes" have a way of becoming unfixed very easily. Regardless of the engagement, whether a project assignment, a management conference, or sustaining counseling, it's crucial to keep the client's long-term benefits in mind.

This sounds rhetorical, I know. Of course, as conscientious consultants we always keep the client's long-term interest in mind. But facts point the other way. Too many consultants, eager to collect fees and move on to the next engagement, propose solutions that seem appropriate now, but lead a client in the wrong direction for the future.

For example, a consultant in the consortium to which I belong took on a business acquisition engagement. The client, a small distributor, wanted to diversify into manufacturing. The consultant performed the search, located three viable candidates, helped negotiate a deal with the client's choice, and arranged acquisition financing. The deal closed. The consultant collected his Lehman scale fee.

A year later the consultant called me, distraught and frightened. The client for which he had performed the acquisition engagement was suing him for breach of contract. The client claimed that the consultant had misrepresented the advantages of making the acquisition. After thinking it through, four months after closing, the president realized that with no manufacturing background, his long-term benefits would be better served by staying in distribution.

Although the court threw out the suit as frivolous, my consulting associate's reputation was besmirched. He had a very difficult time landing his next M & A engagement. It eventually took about a year. Now he insists on a hold harmless clause in every engagement contract.

Sophisticated managers in today's business world increasingly realize that long-term growth takes precedence over short-term profits. Yes, some companies still follow the latter course, but the smart ones, the ones you want to go after as clients, recognize the fallacy of short-term objectives. If nothing else, the Japanese taught us the value of a long-term view when making foreign investments.

An increasing number of companies realize that long-term solutions are worth a lot more than short-term fixes, which is precisely why consultants who recognize this shift in emphasis have increased their fees substantially. More on fee structures in later chapters when exploring specific growth market niches.

PRIMARY CONSULTING SKILLS

Focusing on specific market niches that yield the highest growth potential over the next decade sounds great in theory, but what if your skills don't match market demand? Technology, competition, and government policy create a constantly changing panorama of business innovations demanding new approaches to business management and new solutions to business problems.

During the 1950s and early 1960s, an onslaught of new methodologies met the demand for improved manufacturing and office efficiency. Consultants became efficiency experts, advising clients about productivity measurements, cost analyses, and budgetary techniques. In the late 1960s and early 1970s, as affordable mainframe computers became popular, the Oliver Wight/IBM computer-based production and inventory control systems, "PICS," and later "MAPICS" and "COPICS" configurations brought consultants by the thousands to seminars, conferences, and classrooms to learn these revolutionary techniques.

The rise of the Arab oil states in the 1970s forced renewed emphasis on energy conservation and alternate energy sources, bringing a new cadre of engineers to consulting ranks. Companies began to look to the future, and strategic planning and forecasting model simulation arose as buzzwords in consulting circles. The advent of a new generation of computer technology brought a flock of small business start-ups which encouraged consultants to become adept at sourcing venture capital as a new financing tool.

The booming 1980s brought a wealth of new market niches to the consulting industry. Once again the defense build-up created demand for experts in government contracting. The merger and acquisition frenzy brought a wealth of business to consultants expert in this specialty. Emulating successful Japanese competitors, companies wanted help installing just-in-time receiving and delivery procedures and quality circles. The manufacturing sector succumbed to international competition and service industries arose. Consultants shifted gears to this new, rapid growth segment.

Later in the decade, exporting and importing became passwords to success. Trading companies and export management companies blossomed. Traditional consultants scurried to learn the tricks of the trade lest newer, more progressive advisors steal these new markets.

In the early 1990s, shifts in social concerns brought renewed emphasis on solving industrial environmental problems. Companies learned to meet competition from the Japanese and other foreign competitors head-on by establishing manufacturing and sales facilities in foreign lands. Recessionary pressures forced companies to evolve new methods for solving declining sales and profits. Consul-

ability more common in women make the difference between a resoundingly successful engagement and a mediocre one.

As we all know, management consulting is about as pure a service business as one can find. With the exception of "name" consulting firms such as McKinsey, Andersen Consulting, and the Boston Consulting Group, consultants get and keep clients primarily because of personal relationships. Selling tactics liberally laced with the personal touch bring clients in. A bonding, a personal relationship between consultant and client personnel, keeps them.

Not infrequently, nurturing such a relationship requires a high degree of perceptive intuition. Clients rarely identify their problems correctly. They hardly ever relate the entire story of what caused the problem in the first place. And few, if any, business owners and managers take the time to grasp the motivations and fears of their employees.

Successful consultants perceive the answers as the engagement progresses. Most of these perceptions generate from talking and mixing with client employees, customers, suppliers, and bankers. I have worked hard for years trying to hone my perceptive abilities. On the other hand, I have known several female consultants who analyze a client's problems correctly at the first meeting.

A good friend who participated in our consortium tackled the installation of a local area network (LAN) computer installation while I worked on a new strategic planning process with the CEO, who also owned 51 percent of the company's stock. I wasn't getting very far and couldn't understand what I had missed. The CEO was becoming more and more frustrated.

I asked Mary Sue to join us for lunch and that evening asked her impression. "It seems to me that Bob is stone-walling your efforts because he is afraid his son will force him out if the company becomes too successful." I picked up on her cue and the next day began structuring a new board of directors voting arrangement that would ensure the CEO remained in control. After that, the strategic planning process moved smoothly ahead.

Another case involved the English division of a transnational advertising firm. Three consulting firms, two American and one British, were bidding for the job that involved assisting the company to open new branches in Paris and Copenhagen. The managing director influenced the board's decision to hire a small New York firm run by D.J. Clapt. Mrs. Clapt told me at a seminar we both attended that the managing director stated that she had hired Mrs. Clapt, because she felt a woman could more efficiently recruit management personnel for the new branch.

Although we all try hard not to let sexism influence our business decisions, the fact is that it does. Fortunately for the consulting industry, there seems to be as much discrimination in favor of women as against. As social consciousness accelerates in the decade ahead, and long-term relationships become more important than quick-fix advice, sensitivity and perceptive ability should rank at or near the top of a consultant's skills. This makes it inevitable that women will be just as successful, or more successful, than their male counterparts.

GROWTH MARKETS FOR THE DECADE AHEAD

Government economists, rain makers, and fortunetellers have one thing in common: their predictions for the future are usually wrong. Unlike these soothsayers, I do not guarantee that these are the only consulting opportunities over the next decade, or that all will necessarily enjoy the same rate of growth. However, nothing in the business world is certain. The best we can do is apply logical analyses to existing conditions in an effort to predict future trends. The macro changes discussed earlier point to several consulting markets that have already begun to explode and will probably continue on this track for several years to come. The following summarizes six categories of markets that offer the greatest opportunities.

Specialty and Technical Projects

An unlimited number of niche markets exist within the broad heading of specialty and technical projects. Some require special training, such as environmental compliance, systems design and implementation, financial forecasting, and labor contract negotiations. Others demand a more general management background, such as personnel recruiting, market research, evaluating product line profitability, and developing potential actions for gaining competitive advantage. Skills for other types of engagements such as business acquisition and divestiture work and corporate restructuring depend upon specific contacts from your data base.

Regardless of the specialty or technical expertise, engagements in these niche markets all have similar characteristics.

1. The work is definable. Each project has a beginning and an end.
2. The consultant performs specific activities to implement the project and sees it through to its conclusion.
3. Because of relatively long periods of active participation, a consultant can only manage two or three engagements simultaneously.
4. A consultant's organization must handle marketing activities while the consultant is in the field.
5. These are "one-shot" engagements, without any need for ongoing consultation.
6. Repeat business does not follow.
7. Fees are structured for the project. Maximum, not-to-exceed limits can be included if you use hourly rates. In some cases, consultants charge contingent fees.
8. A specific, definitive scope contract defines what the end result of the project will be and approximately how long it will take to accomplish.
9. Production involves constant interfacing with lower echelon employees in the client organization.
10. Nearly all work is performed at the client's location.

General Management

As with project engagements, an unlimited number of specific niche markets fall under the heading of general management consulting. Examples of this type of engagement include strategic planning, organization development, and employee motivation programs. Consultant's draw upon previous experience as employees or from other engagements for appropriate skills to handle the assignment.

The characteristics of general management engagements are:

1. They extend over long time periods. Many evolve into on-going relationships.
2. Without a specific end to the assignment, scope contracts must be general rather than specific.
3. The consultant remains in a coordination and evaluation role. Implementation is handled by the client.
4. Several engagements can be managed simultaneously. Marketing can be accomplished along with production.
5. Consulting fees are based on hourly rates higher than those charged for project engagements.
6. Because of the on-going relationship, other assignments often evolve from the same client.
7. Production involves interface with business owners in smaller companies and top executives in larger clients.
8. Work is performed at client facility, consultant's office, and other mutually agreed upon locations.

International Consulting

International consulting requires a unique combination of marketing, production, organization, and fee setting. Of all the cutting-edge consulting markets, international consulting remains the most difficult to enter. In addition, the work is the most difficult to perform. International consulting skills cannot be learned from books or in classrooms. They must be learned from experience in the international sphere, and that means an apprentice period.

On the flip side, international consulting offers the highest fees in the consulting business and the greatest opportunities for long-lasting, growth engagements. International consulting involves general management assignments such as strategic planning, organization development, and government interface. It also entails specific projects such as personnel recruiting, site location, financing, market/customer research, and sourcing and negotiating contracts with joint venture partners.

The characteristics of international consulting are:

1. The work entails long-term engagements.

consultant, but he didn't have the capability to handle general management assignments.

Before zeroing in on specific market niches it pays to take a look at what type of consulting business you have, where it is located, how it is organized, and what limitations your life style and skills impose.

LOCATION, STRUCTURE, AND MOBILITY

Before going further, I should clarify my view of management consulting. Contrary to opinions expressed by consulting trade organizations and current consulting literature, consulting is a business, not a profession.

A profession requires proof of technical expertise. It requires a set of standards against which a practitioner can be judged by the public. Most professions require an entrance exam and licensing or certification from an authoritative group, usually a state agency. Professionals who do not abide by the standards can be prohibited from further practice. With standards and regulatory requirements, the public expects certain levels of proficiency when engaging the professional.

Management consulting exhibits none of these characteristics. Anyone can start a management consulting business. No rule-setting body determines performance standards. There is no license to revoke when performance is sub-par, no entrance exam to pass as evidence of technical proficiency, no education requirement. Clients take a gamble every time they hire management consultants.

Granted, certain categories of consultants are licensed, such as those specializing in engineering disciplines. Others call themselves consultants, such as psychologists, pension counselors, and insurance brokers, and many of these are licensed. However, management consultants remain free to come and go as they please and to set their own standards of performance.

Therefore, without standards, regulations, education requirements, or licensing, it seems to me that management consulting must be considered a business. The only relevance of this distinction relates to evaluating competition. From a client's perspective it takes on more importance, especially in the years ahead as consultants are expected to implement as well as advise.

To return to variations in consulting businesses, the type of consulting firm determines to a large extent its capabilities for serving specific market niches. Three organizational characteristics influence the likelihood of success in any given market:

1. Location of the firm
2. Structure of the firm
3. Mobility of consultants

Location of Firm

Although the location of a consulting firm is not crucial to picking market niches, it is important. Firms located in major metropolitan areas have far greater access to financial and market resources than firms located in rural areas or small towns. Metropolitan firms also have access to better market intelligence and a wider range of local contacts. Recruiting qualified personnel and establishing networks with other consultants continue to be much easier in larger communities.

On the other hand, smaller clients in the Midwest or the South generally employ consultants for a wider range of engagements than companies of similar size in metropolitan areas. Competition is certainly less in smaller towns. Frequently, one or two major companies predominate. Landing an engagement with one of these could certainly enhance continuing assignments.

Of the hot new markets examined in this book, only international consulting and M & A work seem to be materially affected by a consulting firm's location. Since only a limited number of cities have direct overseas flights, transportation cost and travel time are greatly improved by beginning and ending at one of these terminals.

For the same reason, most clients interested in international consultants seem to be located in or near a city with convenient overseas transportation. Financial and marketing assistance is also more prevalent in larger cities, especially New York, Chicago, Los Angeles, and Washington, DC.

A substantial part of M & A consulting work involves researching data banks, locating viable buyers and sellers, and sourcing acquisition financing. Each of these steps can be done more efficiently in close proximity to metropolitan resources.

Clearly, the number of potential local clients decreases with the size of the community. Other than having fewer clients to solicit, however, for most consulting markets location in a smaller community offers no great disadvantage over larger cities. On the contrary, consultants concentrating in small business work find it much easier to land clients located in smaller towns or rural areas, although the number of prospects remains less.

Structure of Firm

The size of your consulting firm and the way it is organized have a major bearing on the type of engagements to go after. Taking an engagement with a troubled company that requires you to be on the premises eight hours a day, five days a week, precludes working for any other clients, unless, of course another partner can take up the slack. Similarly, when a sole practitioner takes an international assignment requiring an extended overseas trip, who takes care of the rest of the clients?

Clearly, it's very difficult to take an engagement requiring an extended period away from the office when there isn't anyone else to pick up the slack. Networking or loose partnership associations help. Utilizing one of these methods can get other assignments completed, but you can't rely on an outsider to do the marketing. More on this dilemma later in this chapter.

Some consultants get around the problem to a limited degree by employing a secretary to handle administrative and telephone chores and perhaps a junior to take care of minor work loads. Others try to get by with putting other clients on hold during the extended engagement and hoping that they won't disappear before it's over. Sharon did this when she accepted a recruiting engagement that took her to twelve cities in four weeks. Four weeks is not a very long time to be gone; yet upon returning she found that a competitor with three partners had convinced one of her major small business clients to change to their firm.

There just isn't any satisfactory answer. Sole practitioners who concentrate on markets that require extended periods away from the office can expect a widely fluctuating client base.

Mobility

In this day and age of flights to everywhere and seventy mile per hour freeways crisscrossing the nation, larger clients think nothing of asking consultants to spend hours, sometimes days traveling to remote plants or sales offices. Neither do they think twice about engaging consultants from a different city, even from across the country. But rarely do these same clients pay a consultant for travel time. Expenses yes; time no.

Servicing remote clients creates a series of problems. For sole practitioners it takes them away from the office, leaving other clients to fend for themselves. As Sharon learned, this can bring disastrous results. Second, long-distance travel is very costly in terms of lost billable hours even when out-of-pocket expenses are covered. Third, an extended travel schedule is tiring, diminishing your ability to handle other jobs. Fourth, frequent cross-country or overseas travel damages your health. And fifth, many people do not like to fly at all.

More than one sole practitioner has found it necessary to form a partnership just to take care of other clients while on an extended travel schedule. Others turn down lucrative opportunities because they cannot or will not travel. Clearly, defining appropriate market niches requires weighing the most likely type of engagement against your mobility.

BACKGROUND AND QUALIFICATIONS

In addition to structuring their firm to meet market demands, consultants must weigh available skills and capabilities to perform specific assignments. Whether a sole practitioner or a partner in a larger firm, a consultant's personal characteristics define what market to go after. Those characteristics that have the most influence over choosing market niches seem to be whether:

- A consultant is oriented toward project work, or more comfortable with continuing management engagements.
- A consulting firm specializes in skills or concentrates in one or more industries.
- A consultant is more comfortable working with top management or with lower-echelon managers.

A good starting point is to look closely at your existing client base and decide if this is what you really want for the future. Consulting firms typically handle either a wide variety of assignments without regard to specialization, or a few narrow niche markets requiring specific technical skills. Larger firms with several partners typically choose the former path. The latter is often the favorite of sole practitioners or small partnerships.

Of course no hard rules exist. Many multi-partner firms specialize in broad markets, such as environmental compliance, government liaison, or personnel recruiting. Larger outplacement firms concentrate solely on this aspect of human relations work. Some sole practitioners continue trying to be all things to all clients. Traditionally, however, multi-partner firms maintain a broad client base while small firms concentrate on one or two specialties.

As we now can see, traditional approaches to management consulting don't work anymore. Clients demand implementation help, not just advice. They look to consultants for technical expertise not available internally. They want help in reaching new markets, domestically and overseas. They need specific assistance for sourcing financing, acquisition candidates, management personnel, and joint venture partners.

An analysis and evaluation of your current client base in terms of meeting long-range growth objectives is a crucial first step in developing an internal strategic plan. Do your specialties match the new market niches? Do you have too many clients to take on major new assignments? Should you let some of your clients go, or should you add to your client base? Does your organization and repertoire of skills match your strategic objectives? Have you concentrated too much in one industry? Do you run the risk of a major loss of business by concentrating on too few clients? Or conversely, are you overloaded with low-fee clients that prevent soliciting quality work?

Obviously, if developing an international consulting business appears attractive but current client demands exceed available production hours, something must give. If a client base consists of two or three major corporations and consulting to small businesses offers lucrative opportunities, different skills must be added. If concentration has been on project engagements and sustaining general management markets look attractive, different credentials must be developed. If you have specialized in M & A work and you want to attack the international finance market, transition engagements might have to be taken. And on and on.

As with any other business, the existing customer base and existing product lines strongly influence the amount of flexibility for change. This, more than any other reason, is causing traditional multi-partner firms to worry about future business.

It's one thing to identify what market niches look prosperous over the next decade. It's quite another to shift an existing client base and consulting skills to qualify in these new markets.

Which is precisely why strategic planning is so important. Without a roadmap it's difficult to know how to get to where you want to go, or to know when you have reached your destination.

Another facet of internal strategic planning focuses on client size.

LARGE CORPORATE CLIENTS OR SMALL BUSINESSES

Those of us who have been in consulting for many years know the vast differences between marketing to and working for large clients as opposed to smaller companies. Strategically, it's necessary to evaluate whether we want to go after market niches controlled by large corporations or whether it would be more beneficial to focus on niches with large numbers of smaller companies. Advantages and disadvantages exist in both camps.

Large Clients

Large corporations typically employ large numbers of highly qualified managers with a wide range of specialized skills. Seldom do large corporations engage consultants because they do not have the talent in-house. On the contrary, many large companies have employees as capable, or more capable of executing the task than the consulting firm being hired. Large corporations use consultants for a variety of reasons but seldom because they don't have the internal talent to do the job themselves.

One reason large companies do hire consultants is to provide independent verification of the conclusions reached by in-house staff.

An operating division might want to modify its production control system and proposes modifications to the corporate office. Consultants verify that the division does indeed need a new system and that the proposed system is the best choice.

Another reason is to break political bottlenecks. The board of directors or the CEO might want a fresh approach to reorganizing a division or department. Division and corporate staff bicker over the best structure. Consultants bring independent ideas to the table that do not put down or adversely affect the political future of management personnel.

A third reason might be that no one within the corporation has the time to devote to the task. A division needs to develop a new financial forecasting model. The controller has the aptitude but remains embroiled in day-to-day projects. A consultant designs the system with the controller's approval.

In most large client engagements, consultants remain advisors rather than doers. Clients know how to solve problems but want consultants to tell them what they already know. Once recommendations are on the table, client personnel take over the implementation.

Marketing to large clients takes on a variety of forms, depending on whether you market for repeat work from an existing client or solicit new clients. For repeat work, the best tactics involve continuing communications with the client representative who brought you in for the first assignment, or with the executive responsible for the division or department within which you performed the work. Letters and phone calls following up on the results of the previous engagement; lunches, ballgames, dinner parties; Christmas cards, announcements of changes in your consulting firm, clippings from publicity releases; a periodic newsletter from your firm, and so on, are typical public relations efforts that bring good results.

Soliciting new clients takes on a different tone. Large companies do not respond well to cold calls, whether in person, by phone, or through the mail. Their attitude seems to be that if you have to use cold calls you must be hurting for business and therefore must not be qualified. A much better approach is to get referrals from corporate lawyers, Big-6 public accounting firms, brokerage houses, bankers, and financial analysts. This involves active participation in business and civic groups to become known to these professionals.

Consultants with technical skills—engineering, scientific, medical—successfully attract large clients by teaching at a university, publishing technical papers, and going on the lecture circuit. These are all time-consuming diversions from a consulting practice, however, and full-time management consultants seldom enjoy this luxury.

Small Clients

Small clients, either private or publicly held, present a completely different picture. Small clients hire consultants to get something done. The last thing a smaller company needs is an expert handing out advice about how to run the business. Small business owners and managers pride themselves on knowing the best way to do that. They won't pay an outsider to tell them how to do a better job, even if they need such advice. Therefore, most engagements with smaller clients involve coordinating or actually performing the implementation of your recommendations.

Managers in smaller companies tend to wear several hats. They clearly lack the specialization common in larger companies. Knowledge of sophisticated, state-of-the-art management tools is usually missing. Consultants must tone down their jargon and recommendations to be understood and accepted. Consulting to smaller companies requires hands-on work, frequently necessitating being away from the office for extended periods.

Fees also tend to be lower. The smaller the client, the less you can charge. Clients may need sophisticated systems, planning, or refinancing, but most can't afford to pay for it. Consultants must use other means to make up for the lower fees. One way is to perform several consulting tasks on one engagement. Another is to enter into an on-going contract with a monthly retainer. Lawyers and public accountants frequently approach the problem this way.

Marketing to smaller clients can be more direct than to large companies. Direct mailings, seminars, and publications all work well. Working through local commercial banks also brings results. The smaller the company the more likely it will need financial help. In certain parts of the country, tying into local banks can bring more referrals than any other source. Chapter 10 covers a variety of other marketing techniques to attract small business clients.

MARKETING VERSUS PRODUCTION

All sole practitioners or small partnerships face the dilemma of segregating marketing hours for new business from those needed to perform engagements. Sole practitioners have an especially difficult time taking extended engagements. Without someone minding the store it's hard to take off for three or four weeks to source financing for a client in Europe or Asia. It's just as difficult to take a turnaround engagement requiring daily management of one or more client operating departments.

I have never found an easy answer to this dilemma, other than asking a consortium partner to cover the office. This approach takes care of administrative chores but does little in the marketing area. Many sole practitioners refuse to commit five days a week to any assignment. They insist that four days is the maximum they can spare for any one client and still keep their business afloat. This works well for local clients but misses the boat on traveling engagements.

The production/marketing dilemma is such a serious problem that many sole practitioners form partnerships specifically to cover marketing activities when one or the other is in the field. The choice of one or more market niches depends to a large extent on whether some type of formal or loose partnership arrangement can be worked out. Chapter 4 examines several forms of associations to mitigate this problem.

STRATEGIC LIFE STYLE OBJECTIVES

It should go without saying that it doesn't make sense to focus on market niches that require activities detrimental to a person's chosen life style. Why would a mother with young children specialize in international consulting that repeatedly takes her away from home for extended periods?

Why would a person committed to weekly civic responsibilities solicit extended management turnaround engagements?

Why would someone who enjoys corporate political battlefields focus on small businesses? Or conversely, why would someone with a life time in small business want to get involved with large corporate clients?

Why would a consultant who feels strongly about social issues market to companies deliberately polluting or otherwise destroying the environment? Or a person opposed to smoking or alcohol take on tobacco or liquor clients?

Good questions. No simple answers. Consultants seem to make the same errors time and again.

Royce fell into this trap while trying to build a consulting business after being laid off by Exxon. Bitter and disenchanted with corporate life, he saw consulting as a chance to become a true entrepreneur. With an extensive background in the petroleum industry he used contacts at Exxon to get his first consulting engagement assisting with a distribution site selection for a division of ITT.

In no time Royce became embroiled in internal politics, which he hated. When the assignment was completed, the division manager refused to give Royce a reference citing an "attitude problem." This consultant is still trying to make a go of it with large corporations, even though he intensely dislikes the work environment.

Once again, without a well-conceived strategic plan to attract those clients and engagements that meet our objectives, we fall into the age-old habit of taking whatever work comes over the transom. It's bad enough to get involved in jobs that don't match our organization or capabilities. We create a double-barreled problem when we head into markets in direct conflict with our personal life style and beliefs.

One of the advantages of being in the management consulting business is that we can pick and choose those markets and clients that fit our abilities and objectives. Concentrate on those markets that you enjoy and that you can handle. Let the competition take the rest.

A KNOWLEDGE BANK

Each sizzling market of the next decade requires specific skills and talent. Some demand more of a technical background than others, such as environmental compliance. Others draw on previous experience at the corporate level, such as organization development. Still others look to skills in general management, business start-ups, or global finance.

Few consultants have the resources or the inclination to return to college for another degree. By the time we reach the consulting level, however, most of us have a fairly substantial background in a variety of business disciplines. Age has a lot to do with it. Obviously, older consultants have more exposure to a greater variety of business situations than younger consultants.

A wide array of sources exists to refresh old skills or to enable learning enough about new skills to put them into practice, without the need to go after another degree. Technical seminars and conferences are a great way to bring dusty skills to current levels. Periodically, I attend various tax seminars just to learn what new regulations have evolved since the last time around. The Conference Board (Princeton, NJ) and the American Management Association offer a variety of seminars geared to practically any subject you might want.

Most cities and every state sponsor periodic seminars covering the gamut of subjects from starting a business, to exporting, to business finance, to international trade. By the way, seminars and conferences are great places to meet other consultants, professional accountants and lawyers, even potential new clients. I have picked up more than one client through introductions made at technical seminars.

Trade shows are another interesting way to find out what's happening in a specific industry. These can be valuable in providing background information for general management engagements. It always looks good to clients when you know something special about their industry.

Community colleges frequently offer adult education courses in basic business skills—accounting, marketing, budgeting, traffic and so on, although I have yet to hear of one advanced enough to be of much help building consulting skills. The Department of Commerce publishes hundreds of bulletins pertaining to specific business topics. The Small Business Administration does the same. Local offices of both stock most of their literature. Eximbank in Washington will send bundles of exporting literature on request.

Trade associations also publish periodicals and newsletters. Any good library maintains reference works listing the names and addresses of trade associations throughout the country. It's amazing how many specialized business niches are supported by their own trade organization.

I find specialized magazines and other periodicals extremely beneficial for keeping abreast of current developments and new techniques in a variety of areas. For international trade I recommend *World Trader* (Taipan Press, Inc., Irvine, CA), *The Banker* (Financial Times, London), *Current History* (Current History, Inc., Philadelphia), *Export Today* (Washington, DC.), and *Foreign Affairs* (Council on Foreign Relations, Inc., New York).

The Secured Lender magazine should be must reading for consultants focusing on troubled companies. Several computer magazines, such as *PC World* keep you up to date on what's happening in that arena. *Taxes, The Tax Magazine* (CCH, Chicago) and the newsletter, *Tax Hotline* (Boardroom Reports, Inc., New York) do an excellent job of providing tax tips and planning ideas.

In addition to periodicals, a boatload of business books is published every year. Write to the major business book publishers for their current catalogs and I guarantee you'll find something pertaining to your area of interest. The major publishers are: Prentice-Hall; Simon & Schuster; McGraw-Hill; Wiley & Sons; Richard D. Irwin; Bob Adams; HarperBusiness; and AMACOM (American Management Association).

Computer data banks maintain a wealth of information about virtually any subject. If you have a computer telecommunications hookup you can download from any one of several data base companies listed in any city telephone directory, usually under "Information Bureaus."

If all else fails and you can't locate appropriate information in your field of interest, the trusty reference desk of your local library should put you on the trail of volumes of reference works. I have started more than one assignment in the library. I wouldn't be surprised if management consultants frequent library reference desks more than anyone else.

3 *Organizing and Getting Up to Speed*

This chapter is for new consultants. It has little relevance for those already established and operating a prosperous, growing business. On the other hand, if your business isn't as prosperous as you would like or isn't matching your expectations for growth, some of the ideas in this chapter might help.

A consulting firm is probably the easiest and least costly business to start-up. All you need is a telephone, table, and chair, and a little later some letterhead and business cards. An inexpensive computer with word processing can be invaluable. Nothing else. No fax machine, no copier, no fancy furniture.

In the beginning it's foolish to rent office space. You can always meet prospective clients in their office, a restaurant, or your club. Use some spare space in your home as a makeshift office: a spare bedroom, a basement, or anywhere you can find a free corner.

THAT'S ALL! Wait until the clients come before jumping to executive suite status.

Before worrying about how to equip an office, it's a good idea to give some thought to organizing your business. Should you operate as a sole proprietorship or a corporation? Should you try to find partners or go it alone? What liability protection do you need? How about taxes? Will the market niches you go after influence how to organize the business?

It might seem premature to worry about such matters before the first client walks in the door, but it really isn't. Under certain circumstances, teaming up with a partner works better if done before starting a marketing effort. Office layout, equipment needs, and possibly employee recruiting follow closely on the heels of the first few clients. However, a liability protection program and tax planning should be implemented immediately.

LIABILITY PROTECTION

If a truism exists in today's business world it is that at one time or another every one of us will be sued in a court of law. The time to begin protecting your income, personal assets, and business is now, right in the beginning, before anyone has a chance to hurt you. An insurance package to cover business liability, fire and casualty, loss caused by vandalism, theft, or other expropriation of property should be taken out immediately, if you can afford it.

Insurance is expensive, however. Without a continuing client base it's difficult to justify spending large amounts on coverage you may not need for some time. A summary of recommended insurance coverage appears near the end of this chapter, for those so inclined.

Operating a business under a corporate umbrella may not afford complete protection but it's a good start. Corporations are not lawsuit-proof. Courts easily pierce the corporate shield under certain circumstance. Nevertheless, a corporation provides greater protection than any other form of business structure.

Several states have made it very easy and inexpensive to form a corporation. Delaware and Nevada remain the best. Contrary to what the legal profession would have us believe, an attorney is definitely not necessary to form a corporation, especially in Delaware. Call the Company Corporation in Wilmington, Delaware, or any number of other incorporating companies, and within a week or so, you'll have a corporation, complete with corporate seal, minute book, and stock certificates, all for under $200. If Delaware isn't attractive, these companies will incorporate your business in the state of your choice.

Once incorporated, the next step should be to implement a personal asset protection plan, if you don't already have one in place.

PARTNERSHIP OR SOLO

The next question to address is whether it makes sense to find another consultant with whom to form a partnership or some other type of association. As described in Chapter 2, significant advantages arise in having two or more partners when going after business in those market niches requiring significant time away from the office. On the other hand, all partners must pull their share of fees or it becomes uneconomical.

The decision rests on the relative importance of five areas:

1. Marketing effort
2. Work load
3. Fee volume
4. Administrative overhead
5. Business management

Marketing

Without any doubt the biggest problem faced by beginning consultants is implementing an effective marketing campaign while keeping sufficient hours open for production. Established consultants experience the dilemma in reverse: how to restrict production hours in order to have enough time to market new clients. Either way, a sole practitioner has a tough time allocating time between marketing and production.

I don't know of any practicing consultant who has solved this problem without bringing a second party into the business. Some consultants who concentrate on market niches requiring a great deal of low-fee work, such as consulting to small businesses, get by with office clerical help. A secretary, bookkeeper, or data entry clerk can cover the phone, handle most administrative chores, and still have time for billable hours such as keeping a client's books or entering client computer data.

Some consultants elect to hire low-level clerical help as full time employees (or independent contractors). This works fine as long as enough low-fee work exists to charge at least 75 percent of their time to client hours, or if a large enough client base exists to warrant overhead personnel. As an alternate and less costly method, hire independent contractors on an "as needed" basis.

Many retirees, homemakers, and college students are eager for the opportunity to earn a few dollars part-time. Small public accounting, bookkeeping, and tax firms also welcome additional work during slack periods. Regardless of the route chosen, having someone to cover the office and pick up low-fee production work can free sufficient time to engage in an on-going marketing campaign.

Consultants who focus on markets that demand travel time or sustained management time at a client's location can't get by with clerical help. Only two ways exist to allocate sufficient time to a marketing effort: (1) restrict billable hours to 50 or 60 percent of available hours and spend the balance on administration and marketing, or (2) team up with one or more consultants to share the work load and the marketing. In the latter case a single employee might have to be added to take care of administrative chores. In the beginning part-time help should be sufficient.

Consultants seem to fall into one of three categories:

- Individual performers who prefer to work on their own
- Partners who prefer to work with another consultant
- Team players who prefer to work with several partners

When consultants organize their business along the lines of their personal work preference, they generally stay in business. Those who cross over to a different type of organization frequently fail. It's important to understand which category describes your characteristics and then organize your business accordingly.

When I decided I wanted to begin international consulting I realized I needed a partner to handle the marketing when I was out of the country. I teamed up with one of my consortium members to form a loose partnership, one without a formal partnership agreement. The scheme worked well for about six months, as long as I was overseas.

Once I returned, however, it didn't take long before we were squabbling over billable time, administrative duties, and client allocation. Shortly thereafter we split up. That experience taught me that I was definitely an individual performer and had to structure my business accordingly, even if it meant restricting the number of new clients I could handle.

A good friend specializing in turnarounds and workouts has the opposite characteristics. He works much better with a partner. This consultant spends 60 percent of his time on marketing while his partner allocates the same amount of time to production. A perfect fit.

Team players, on the other hand, usually do better in a larger consulting firm with several partners, sharing both marketing and production loads.

Work Load

Being associated with one or more consultants brings distinct advantages for sharing work loads. Chapter 4 describes the various organization arrangements other than formal partnerships. It should be mentioned that when I speak of partnerships I do not mean a legal partnership as opposed to a corporation. The corporate form is the way to go regardless of the number of partners you have. The term "partnership" as used here refers to a sharing of ownership of the operating business, not its legal form.

Regardless of the type of engagement, one of two conditions invariably arises: the client wants the job completed sooner than originally planned, or we run into situations that we do not have the expertise to handle efficiently. In both cases, having one or more partners to call on for assistance can be a lifesaver.

One of my first turnaround clients was desperately in need of an injection of equity capital. None of my financial sources were interested. Spending twelve hours a day at my client's plant trying to sort out organizational problems, I didn't have time to begin new finance sourcing. I called upon a consortium member with many contacts in the venture capital field. Within two weeks he produced an investor willing to take a 20 percent equity interest in exchange for a cash injection of $1 million.

Fees

It goes without saying that the more billable hours you have, the more income you generate. A good rule of thumb applicable to many market niches states that consultants can bill a maximum of 60 percent of annual available hours. The balance must be allocated to marketing and administration. If you spend more than 60 percent, either marketing or administration activities, or both, suffer.

It doesn't take a mathematical genius to calculate the available hours in a year (1,944 if you take off eight holidays and two weeks for vacation). Sixty percent amounts to 1,166 hours. At a $100 hourly rate, that's maximum gross income of $116,000, assuming you stay busy all year. Typical overhead expenses in a one-person consulting firm with this much work run between 40 and 50 percent. That leaves net income of approximately $65,000, or after-tax cash of $46,000, not a large amount for all that work.

Obviously these factors vary for each consulting business. Engagements performed for a flat fee or a percentage, such as with an M & A job or capital sourcing, normally turn a higher gross income. A high percentage of billable hours to small businesses results in a lower average rate than $100 per hour. Overhead expenses can be reduced below 40 percent. Adequate tax planning often results in taxes of less than 28 percent. Still, as a ballpark figure, take-home pay of $50,000 to $60,000 per year is not unusual for a solo consulting business.

Only two ways exist to permanently increase income: take engagements commanding a higher hourly fee, or combine billable hours and share expenses with a partner.

Setting a fee structure can be tricky. Some market niches such as acquisition and divestiture engagements have widely accepted standards (Lehman Scale formulae). Sustaining management engagements and most of the international jobs command flat weekly or monthly fees. Projects may be billed at a flat amount. Many engagements, however, carry an hourly rate. This rate varies by type of client, complexity, locale, competition, and, of course, what the traffic will bear. Hourly rates comparable to the mid-range for lawyers and CPAs—currently between $75 and $150 per hour—are generally acceptable.

Structuring a flat fee for the entire job gets tricky. I generally estimate how many hours it will take, add 20 percent for contingencies, and price the hours at my hourly rate for that type of work. Some assignments require reduced rates—such as for a small business start-up. Some command a higher than normal rate, such as project work for larger organizations. Flexibility is the key, and in the beginning fees must be structured to what the traffic will bear. Just don't undersell yourself—that's one sure path to failure.

Administration and Business Management

Hours used for administrative chores are clearly nonproductive and must be kept to a minimum. Typing, filing, bookkeeping, filing tax reports, answering the phone, scheduling trips and appointments, and a myriad of other administrative chores can easily get out of hand. I reached the point in my business where the only way I could handle administration was to do most of these chores on weekends. This works for a while, but a steady diet robs a person of much needed R & R and leads to abdication of family responsibility.

It's less expensive in the long run to hire part-time or full-time help to handle administrative chores. Beginning consultants without a client base obviously can't afford such a luxury. They must do the work themselves. Weekends can and should be used to fill the gap until the business develops.

I have been asked many times how long it takes to start a consulting business. Based on my own experience and that of many other consultants, a good rule of thumb seems to be that it takes a full three years to generate a sustaining, living wage. Income should begin flowing within the first year, but it takes another two to reach a sustaining level. If you don't generate at least $20,000 to $30,000 the first year, get out. You're in the wrong business.

When two or more consultants share the same office, overhead expenses do not double. In fact, other than telephone costs, they rarely increase at all. Not only does a partner bring in extra billings without incurring overhead expenses, but a partner also shares in the administrative work load. Clearly, another good reason to join forces.

It's also much easier to manage a consulting business with one or more partners. Disagreements inevitably arise: conflicting opinions about how and when to market, how many hours a job should take, what overhead costs to incur, and so on. Nevertheless, when it comes to business management, two heads are usually better than one.

A partnership presents a better image to clients than a solo consultant. It substantiates a greater number of skills. It eases the burden of administrative chores. It fortifies your contention that the firm will be in existence two, three, four years from now and therefore a client can trust you with long-term assignments. And last, but certainly not least, it increases the amount of capital for running the business. Record keeping is always painful and nonproductive, even for accountants. Accurate record keeping, however, especially of expenses, can significantly reduce your tax burden. Many expenses considered personal for the wage earner are now deductible as business expenses: allocated house expenses for an office, auto expenses, client relations and entertainment, club dues, and so on. Even though painful, record keeping must be done. I have found a modestly priced software package to be the least annoying and most efficient way to get over this hurdle. For several years I used one called "One-Write Plus", put out by Great American Software, Inc., P.O. Box 910, Amherst, NH 03031. It cost about $100. Several others are also available.

THE BIONIC OFFICE

The information age has changed consulting offices. Unfortunately, traditional firms continue to wallow in the morass of large clerical staffs. They refuse to abandon outmoded, slow computers, outdated typewriters, antiquated copiers and dictating equipment, and twenty-year-old visual aids for presentations.

Cutting-edge consultants find a better way. Not only does state-of-the-art office equipment increase the speed and accuracy of client reports, it also reduces the number of employees needed to manage administrative tasks. It almost always pays to join this parade. Learn about new administrative methods and equipment, and then make the investment in time and money to get up and running as fast as possible (i.e., as soon as you can afford it). Some consultants have used bionic offices to create a whole new subsidiary business by selling office services to other small businesses.

Entire books have been published describing the office of the future. Such inclusiveness is impractical here. However, a review of some of the more practical innovations in office procedures might prove helpful. The following summarizes what's available under four headings: records management, communications, marketing and reports, and information retrieval.

Equipment and service costs vary all over the lot. Rapid technological improvements and intense competition force price decreases faster than this book will be published. Therefore, the prices included should not be taken as gospel truth. They are at best midrange quotes at the time of this writing. Nor should this summary be considered to include everything available. Office management technology moves too fast.

Records Management

Consultants tend to get buried in paper: client files, report drafts, canceled checks, correspondence, tax returns and supporting documentation, bookkeeping records, and on and on. It doesn't take long to fill one file cabinet after another, except in bionic offices. Filing cabinets and paper records can be thrown away. They are no longer needed. The personal computer has replaced manual records of all types with convenient, small, and secure discs.

A high quality personal computer capable of doing everything you need can be purchased new for under $3,000. Add another $800 for a high speed, letter quality printer. I prefer top of the line IBM or Compaq computers, and Epson or NEC printers—Hewlett-Packard for laser printing. Others remain loyal to the Apple line. Still others save money by buying clones. The brand is irrelevant as long as it is nationally supported and compatible with your needs.

Several excellent software packages exist for nearly every conceivable application. Software prices again range widely, depending on the brand name and how comprehensive you want the programs to be. Every office should have basic software for accounting, word processing, financial forecasting and analysis, data base storage, desk top publishing, and telecommunications. The first four are used for records management.

Any library carries reference books listing current software by application. The magazine *PC World* does a good job analyzing the advantages and disadvantages of new programs. It also carries a myriad of advertisements for software developers. For those who may need a starting point, the following modestly priced software works well in the average size office:

Accounting—One-Write Plus
Word processing—WordStar 2000
Financial forecasting and analysis—Lotus 123
Data base storage—dBase II
Desk top publishing—Ventura
Telecommunications—Smartcom II

I use both the IBM P/S 2, Model 50 and Compaq Portable computers. All the above software is compatible. It may not be the most powerful software on the market today, nor the least expensive, but it is all compatible with my equipment, I understand how to use it, and it does the job. Other software is just as efficient. This configuration can currently be purchased for less than $3,000.

For those wishing to prepare their own tax returns, several good tax software packages are available. The price runs high, ranging from $1,000 to $8,000, and the software must be updated annually for changes in tax laws and return formats. I prefer to let my CPA spend the money.

All supporting tax documentation can be stored in the data base program, on disc. Accounting records, correspondence copies, draft reports can all be maintained on disc. The data base program is a good place to store client files. In other words, throw out the file cabinets and keep everything on disc. But don't forget to maintain backup copies of all discs and store them away from your office.

Communications

Communications technology has leapfrogged into the 21st century. Facsimile transfer machines costing $4,000 to $10,000 five years ago can now be purchased for less than $1,000, and transmission is twice as fast. Rather than the exception, offices with fax equipment are becoming the rule. Internationally, fax machines are replacing outmoded telex equipment in many developed and developing nations. A person can hardly do business in Europe or Japan anymore without access to a fax.

One limitation still exists for all high-tech communications equipment. Both sending and receiving locations must have reliable electrical service and dependable telephone systems. This forestalls many poor developing nations from acquiring high-tech communications and limits the use of this technology to larger cities in many other developing or Third World countries. Nevertheless, high-speed, inexpensive telecommunication is here to stay.

In addition to a fax, a bionic office should have a compatible telecommunications software package and reliable modem for its PCs. With this capability, you can tie directly into a client's computer system to download data and reports. Concurrently, you can forward data, reports, analyses, forecasts, and a variety of other information direct to a client.

Telecommunications capability also allows direct communication with airlines reservation systems, hotel bookings systems, current news announcements, financial market trends, and a variety of other national and regional computer systems. Naturally, every tie-in costs money, but the time saved frequently makes it worthwhile.

Telecommunications capability is extremely important for consultants involved in international engagements. Not only does it permit direct access to your office back home, it provides another valuable tool for obtaining data and reports from local government and financial circles. More than once, quick access to such information has made the difference between concluding and not concluding a contract negotiation.

Digital telephones (replacing the cellular models) are another example of modern communications technology. Though not especially applicable to an office, the time saved with pocket phones in automobiles, airplanes, and any number of other locations usually more than makes up for their high cost.

Consulting firms with employees, with more than one principal, or with more than one office location, frequently find computer network systems very useful. Each desk top computer feeds into a central processing unit with significantly more calculating and storage capability than individual PCs. Several people can draw from the same data bases or download the same reports whenever they need them.

Two or more offices can be tied into the same central processing unit and draw data at will. Any partner or employee in any office may access client files stored in a data base. Private entry codes provide security by limiting access of central files to those with the proper password.

Marketing and Report Generation

The days of choosing between sloppily prepared reports and spending a fortune on outside design and printing capability have long passed. Desk top publishing software brings professional layout, printing, and report production capability to the bionic office. Depending on the capabilities of your printer, reports can be generated in a full color spectrum, with pictures, logos, diagrams, and graphs.

Desk top publishing also cuts substantial costs from advertising budgets. Full page color ads, brochures, client flyers, newsletters, even letterhead and envelopes complete with logo can be produced with desk top publishing. Many consultants, including myself, have completely abandoned advertising agencies and print shops.

By adding a few inexpensive pieces of low-tech equipment you can prepare complete reports and production copy for media advertising. Two pieces are essential: a small laminating machine to plastic-coat report covers, and a punching machine to install plastic binders.

A high speed copying machine that produces letter quality copies is another essential piece of equipment. I still prefer Xerox, but Ricoh, Canon, and a number of other manufacturers also produce very high quality equipment. For larger offices, it helps to get a copier with collating capability. Also be certain it copies on both sides of a sheet of paper. This saves a bundle on paper costs for lengthy reports.

Many consultants find camcorders useful for videotaping promotion pieces. Local television channels willingly accept such videos for advertising spots. Quality camcorders run under $1,000. This is significantly less expensive than making a TV spot in a studio.

Televideo equipment has been available for several years although marketing efforts to attract the public have fallen flat. Recent innovations, however, in both the telephone and television industries point to higher quality and lower cost equipment in the very near future. Certainly within the next decade, modern offices will be equipped with televideo systems that will make today's conference calls outmoded.

Data Retrieval

Research remains the bane of many consultants. All too often engagements require current data that cannot be gathered except by lengthy research. Searching for acquisition or divestiture targets, uncovering likely customers in foreign markets, isolating financing sources, identifying joint venture partners, and performing market research can be time consuming and many times unbillable. Identifying potential new clients very often requires man-days of research. Untold hours reading, dissecting, and assimilating information from libraries and journals can be spent. Data retrieval services provide the answer.

The Department of Commerce, Digilog, Dun & Bradstreet and many others have compiled enormous data bases of information about everything imaginable. Some federal government data bases can be accessed directly from your computer at very little cost. Private company data bases cost more. Once you locate the appropriate data base for the type of information you need, merely pay the required charge, turn on your computer, and begin downloading.

Data base searches are especially helpful in the M&A business and in international consulting engagements. In fact, it's nearly impossible to penetrate these markets without the use of at least one, and many times several, data bases.

CLIENT CONTRACTS

Some consultants feel more secure with a definitive contract covering every conceivable area of the engagement. Others feel unduly restricted with legally binding contracts. No common ground exists for all consultants for all types of engagements. Certain common sense rules are relevant, however.

It only makes sense to execute a scope agreement that defines what a client wants you to accomplish. Without a scope agreement you can never be sure when the engagement ends or whether you have in fact done what you set out to do for the client. As a minimum, a scope agreement should include the following provisions or clauses, regardless of the type of engagement.

1. *Definition of work to be performed*—a concise statement clarifying precisely what you and the client expect to be accomplished and any restrictions placed on what you do or how you do it.

2. *Fees*—hourly rate, flat fee, or percentage fee. If percentage fee, include definition of what it applies to and how and when the base will be determined. Be sure the agreement states when the fee will be paid—e.g., weekly, monthly, in advance, against a retainer.

3. *Time*—include a range of dates between which the engagement will be completed. For a sustaining management engagement, identify a not-to-exceed deadline.

4. *Hold harmless*—a clause stating that the client will hold you harmless from any liability you might incur as a result of the engagement. This clause is crucial, especially for turnaround clients or government contract jobs.

5. *Best effort*—a clause stating that you will perform your "best efforts" on the engagement. This means that if the client isn't satisfied, at least you have tried your best to bring the results expected.

6. *Out-of-pocket expenses*—reimbursement provision covering all out-of-pocket expenses associated with engagement. Be sure to stipulate whether the client has the right to authorize expenditures before they are made.

These represent the main features of a scope agreement. Obviously they can be extended or abbreviated depending on the circumstances. It's important to get the scope contract executed before beginning to work. Once the engagement has been started, too many situations arise to cause disagreement and the contract may never get signed.

INSURANCE

Every business person needs insurance against catastrophic loss. Unfortunately, consultants seem to be notorious for ignoring such a basic principle. Doctors, lawyers, even architects buy malpractice insurance, assuming they can afford the premiums. Those of us who consult to small businesses continually caution owners to keep their insurance coverage current. Yet when it comes to our own business we tend to be negligent.

Consultants should carry four types of insurance coverage for certain. International consultants need more. The following summarizes the types of insurance you should not be without, as soon as you can afford it.

1. Liability. Although consultants seldom get sued for negligent performance, it does happen. Those who specialize in troubled companies or government contracting are especially susceptible to suits, both from clients and from third parties. Although not as expensive as physicians' malpractice insurance, consultants' liability coverage can count up.

The best approach to keeping the cost down is to structure a "per job" policy with your broker. As you undertake an engagement that could lead to claims of conflict of interest, breach of contract, or other liability claims, merely tell the broker who then initiates the policy. When the danger ends, terminate the coverage.

2. Automobile. Some states have allowed insurance companies to jack the premiums on automobile insurance so high that a person can hardly afford to own a car. Yet consultants must have mobility, therefore a car, therefore automobile insurance. If you have one or more partners, then by all means look at fleet coverage. It could be much cheaper than an individual policy. If a sole practitioner, consider the possibility of joining forces with other solo consultants, public accountants, or lawyers in the area specifically to qualify for fleet coverage.

3. Property and casualty. Consultants normally do not have high value equipment to insure against fire or other hazards. They do, however, have a lot of hours tied up in client work that resides in files, either computer files or manual files. A catastrophic loss of these files could easily put you out of business. Therefore, it only makes sense to carry adequate coverage. Your homeowners policy may or may not be sufficient. Not only should you consider fire and casualty coverage, but business interruption as well, although these policies are expensive.

4. *Health and life.* Certainly larger firms carry employee group health and life coverages. Solo consultants should also. Life insurance is straightforward: carry what you can afford. Non-group health insurance premiums have become totally exorbitant. I don't know of anyone who can afford individual policies, at least not when starting a business.

Small business groups policies offer a possible alternative. Several companies offer health coverage in varying amounts to small business owners. One-person businesses qualify, as long as you really are in business and not an employee. The best source of information for contacting these companies continues to be local business groups, such as the chamber of commerce. If that doesn't work, use the telephone book and start calling around. As a side issue, if you elect to enter the international consulting market, be aware that many health policies do not extend to overseas locations. Be sure to ask your insurance agent.

5. *Disability income.* Disability income coverage presents a dilemma for consultants. If you have been in business for a while to substantiate an average annual income, coverage is available. Starting out without an income record makes it a bit iffy. In any case, disability income coverage is extremely expensive. Unless you have a consuming reason for it, such as substantial financial commitments, it's probably a good idea to forget about it, although many disagree and swear by this coverage regardless of cost.

6. *Travel.* Accidental death and dismemberment policies are relatively inexpensive, but most do not cover international travel. You can always buy coverage at airports, but the cost is exorbitant. If you carry an American Express card try their coverage. It does extend to overseas travel and seems to be reasonably priced. Some Visa and MasterCard companies also offer similar coverage. The American Automobile Association sells reasonably priced coverage for automobile travel. For an extra premium, it also extends coverage overseas.

Neither a bionic office, insurance coverage, or the structure of your business will make you a million dollars, but getting set up properly in the beginning can eliminate a lot of headaches later on. We all have a tendency, at least in the beginning, to spend too much time worrying about administrative details.

It really doesn't make any difference to clients whether you operate out of a forty-second floor executive suite or your basement. Clients certainly don't care what type of insurance you carry. As long as you produce quality work they don't care whether you use computers, copiers, or any other modern office equipment. And I have never known of a consulting firm landing an important new client as a result of the color or design of letterheads or brochures.

On the other hand, we have enough difficulty keeping administrative work to a minimum and a bionic office certainly helps. Many consultants have been in business for years without carrying liability insurance or worrying about schemes to protect their assets. But all it takes is one lawsuit and any small business can be wiped out—including a consulting business. It just doesn't make sense to ignore these few simple steps that might, in the long run, save you millions of dollars, and at a minimum make life a little easier.

4 Getting and Keeping Clients

Consultants complain as much about how difficult it is to get new clients as they do about being overworked and underpaid. They don't mean that they can't get ANY clients. They mean that the work they get isn't the type they really want, or that they can't bill as much as they think the job is worth. Getting the right clients at the right fee seems to be an occupational hazard for both new and experienced consultants. As pointed out in earlier chapters, a lack of internal strategic planning creates this condition as much as anything else.

The underlying principle of sound strategic planning is to define precisely the mission of the company. In consulting, that means defining what skills and knowledge you have to sell and identifying those long-term growth markets that demand such expertise. The more definitive one can be, the higher the probability of attracting the right clients.

Most of us have substantial knowledge in more than one discipline. In certain types of engagements it is not enough to be competent, however: one must be an expert. In 1982 Hubert Bermont stated succinctly in his book *The Complete Consultant*: "I find that most people who aspire to consultancy are totally unaware that they have to be *tops* in their field to qualify. *Mere competence is not enough.* They do not understand that clients will not pay for mediocrity or for the fact that a self-proclaimed consultant (as we all are) must have more going for him or her than five or ten years in the field."

The chosen few whose superiority or expertise in specialized market niches is measurable by public or professional recognition (and who have in fact attained such recognition) have no difficulty getting as many of the right type of clients as they want. Unfortunately, most consulting markets cannot be so defined; and most of us have not achieved such recognition as renowned experts.

On the other hand, we can all avoid the cloak of mediocrity. Bermont is totally correct when he acknowledges that mediocrity, or mere tenure in a particular field, is not enough to qualify a consultant. It takes more than that. It takes verifiable credentials of accomplishment to sell skills to clients. It takes a level of credibility to inspire a client's confidence that we know what we are talking about. And it requires communicating this knowledge base to the marketplace.

Since a consultant's credentials and credibility are valuable only if they relate to skills demanded by the market, the starting point is to identify what we have to sell that is marketable. I hate the time-worn phrase "self-evaluation." Books and articles giving advice about how to be a successful consultant are full of checklists and questionnaires for performing "self-evaluations." I'm guilty myself. Such tripe begs the question. We all know what we do well and what we stumble over. We try to sell the former and hide the latter. Such is life in the consulting business.

Once you identify which pieces of your knowledge base are marketable it's time to move on to implementing a marketing program that meets your strategic objectives.

DEVELOPING CREDENTIALS

If one facet of management consulting sets the business apart from other entrepreneurial pursuits it is the overriding emphasis on marketing. Other business owners enjoy the option of passing the selling responsibility to employees with outstanding sales aptitude. They may not know how to manufacture the product, or perform the service they sell, but they know how to get orders. Consultants, on the other hand, have nothing to sell but themselves. No employee or outsider can do the job for us. We must do it ourselves.

Far too many ex-executives enter consulting ranks with a wealth of valuable management and technical talent but a dearth of sales ability. They struggle to make a go of consulting, sometimes for years, but never quite seem to make it, never quite reach the pinnacle of their ability.

An honest assessment of many multi-partner firms that find their client base disintegrating before their eyes would point the finger at the partners' inability to sell their services. New consultants all too often believe that by calling themselves consultants and running a few promotional spots clients will beat a path to their doorstep. Seldom do such tactics work. Consultants must get out in the field and peddle their wares or they won't last very long.

As a starting point, new or experienced consultants must establish undeniable credentials in their particular specialty. Public recognition goes a long way toward opening client doors. Acknowledged expertise smoothes the road to new clients even if you lack selling flair. True, strong marketing efforts are still required. Nothing substitutes for active solicitation. However, without publicly recognized credentials, marketing difficulties escalate geometrically.

How does a person establish specialist credentials? For some it takes years. Others accomplish the feat in short order. No pat answer applies to everyone. Each must search out the most effective means recognizing personal, geographical, and market limitations.

Obviously, if your skills can be certified, then by all means get the certification: a license, award, professional designation, education degree, and so on. Clients love to see a string of letters after your name. If certification doesn't apply, join some authoritative trade or professional organizations serving your specialty. It always looks good to have a few memberships tacked on to your letterhead.

A defined, high-impact publicity program that promotes you as a master in your field works wonders. A wide variety of publicity means can be employed. If you aren't adept at setting up the appointments, hire a small publicity firm to do it for you. This gets expensive, but is a small price to pay for the recognition it brings.

A publicity program establishes your credentials by promoting you as an authority, an advocate, a supporter, or all three.

Become an Authority

To become known as an authority you have to convince the public how much you know about something. Your audience probably doesn't know as much about the subject as you do; therefore, keep your presentations simple, but with enough authoritative-sounding jargon to get the point across. Here are some ideas:

1. Write a book about your specialty (this works wonders if you can find a marketing-oriented publisher!).
2. Write articles for business and trade magazines.
3. Publish a newsletter with current developments in your field (but postage is expensive).
4. Conduct an adult evening school course in a related field.
5. Present your own seminar on a topic related to your marketable skills.
6. Participate in trade conferences and shows as a speaker or panelist.
7. Get on the lecture circuit (hard to get started without previously established credentials).
8. Teach part-time at a local college.
9. Volunteer consulting services to a local SBA office (but don't get involved with the SCORE organization).

Become an Advocate

An advocate takes a stand for something—public duty, human rights, social responsibility, the environment; or against something—drugs, poverty, corporate greed, pollution, taxes. Although becoming an advocate doesn't directly establish consulting credentials, indirectly it does. By expressing your views on a public topic you demonstrate your knowledge and experience in the specific subject. More important, audience attention gets focused on you as an individual.

When you call on a potential client and you get the remark, "Didn't I see you on television last week? You really presented good arguments," you'll know how effective advocacy can be. Of course, advocates also run the risk of offending. Nevertheless, effective public imaging must present you as strong, confident, and experienced, willing and able to argue your views persuasively, whether offensive or not.

Some positive ways to get public exposure as an advocate are:

1. Get on a TV talk show.
2. Be interviewed on network radio.
3. Get quoted in newspaper and magazine articles.
4. Write "letters to the editor" for your local newspaper.
5. Participate actively in civic, community, and social consciousness organizations.
6. Donate your time to youth groups, poverty rehabilitation programs, elderly assistance groups, or literacy training.
7. Organize community action groups—recycling projects, governmental awareness programs, anti-crime groups, crisis assistance, or youth involvement.

Become a Supporter

Becoming a supporter carries the same risks of offending as advocacy. But then, you can't please everyone all the time, just like you can't sell all consulting services to all types of clients. Consultants cannot afford to offend too many people, however, so it pays to carefully pick and choose what to support and how vociferous to become.

As with advocacy, publicly supporting something or someone doesn't directly establish consulting credentials in the market niches you're after, but it does bring you into contact with influential people who can indirectly point you to clients. I have found that extending support in the area of public politics (as opposed to corporate politics) works extremely well for certain market niches. I doubt that I could have pierced either government contracting or international markets without reciprocal support from public figures.

Here are a few ideas for becoming a supporter that other consultants have used effectively:

1. Write opinion letters to your congressional representatives—both senators and congressmen(women).
2. Run for local office on a party ticket.
3. Get elected (or appointed) to the local school board or planning commission.

4. Get to know top level bureaucrats in the Washington offices of the SBA, Eximbank, Department of Commerce agencies, procurement bureaus.

5. Appear on TV and radio in support of local officials running for elected office.

6. Acknowledge support for state representatives when specific issues come up for vote.

7. Write a commentary for the Ed-Op page of your local newspaper.

Using the three-pronged attack—becoming an authority, an advocate, and a supporter—seems to bring better results than choosing one over the other. In addition to developing credentials and contacts, an effective publicity or public relations program firmly relays your image as a person who is honest and forthright and who possesses all those good attributes that everyone admires but few of us really have. This can be as important as establishing credentials once you get in the door to talk to a prospective client.

PERSONAL DEMEANOR

We cannot all be super sales people. Those fortunate few have the knack for closing an order once they get in a client's door. The rest of us struggle with other means. If you have successfully overcome the technical proficiency hurdle, the next step is to convince the prospective client that you conduct yourself in a professional manner. A consultant's demeanor at the first meeting very often determines whether an engagement results or whether the meeting is a waste of time.

Regardless of which management level your contact may be in the company's organization, it's extremely important to treat the person professionally. This means dressing the part. It also means exhibiting all those good characteristics you have tried so hard to establish publicly—honesty, loyalty, thoroughness, confidence, commitment, and confidentiality.

Honesty, loyalty, and thoroughness stand without comment. The three Cs, however, bear closer scrutiny.

Clients want to be certain that consultants are totally confident, not only in their ability to do the work, but that the results of the engagement will be what the client expects. Confidence cannot be stated: it must be felt. It's easy to tell if people have confidence in what they do, even on the phone. An air of expectancy, enthusiasm, assurance leaps out. Conversely, it's just as easy to spot lack of confidence.

Consultants must exude confidence. Use whatever means are necessary to convey to the client that you are the best and only person to do the job. No one else can come close to producing the results that the client needs. For some engagements I have gone as far as guaranteeing the results the client expects. If not satisfied, I guarantee to keep working at the assignment until the client is happy, at no additional cost.

Clients also want to know that consultants will be committed to the engagement. The last thing a client wants to hear is that another client takes precedence over his engagement. Clients like to feel that they are number one in your repertoire. Yes, they want to know that you have many other clients as proof of your abilities. But once you begin their assignment, they want everything else put aside. They want your full, undivided, committed attention.

Total confidentiality is a must. Clients must be assured that the financial, product, market, competition, design, and other information you glean from their business remains sealed in your files. Successful consultants learn early in the game to respect a client's privacy. Complete and total confidentiality must be conveyed strongly and persuasively at the first meeting.

Certainly "personal chemistry" is an overworked cliché. Nevertheless, when it comes to repeat business or future references, as experienced consultants we know that the best results come from a CEO, business owner, or client manager with whom we have established a good rapport, a meeting of the minds, a good personal chemistry.

ADVERTISING YOUR WARES

Personal service business owners, including consultants, are more likely to use publicity and public relations programs than advertising to seek new clients. Many people continue to wince when they see advertisements from physicians, lawyers, financial planners, public accountants, psychologists, and others regarded as professionals. Traditionally, it seems somehow unprofessional to blatantly advertise personal services, to actually solicit business.

Caught in the trap of thinking of themselves as professionals, many management consultants suffer the same malady. However, in California and some of the other more forward-thinking areas of the country, consultants are learning fast that advertising does bring clients and that clients don't regard such tactics as unprofessional, providing the advertisement is done in good taste. Even in the traditionally conservative Philadelphia area a few brave souls seek clients through advertising.

The secret, of course, is to come up with tasteful campaigns that get the message across without being offensive. Spot television commercials, conservative newspaper spreads, and well-placed mailings are a few examples consultants use effectively.

Most consultants do not seem very adept at advertising their own wares. It's easy to critique a client's advertising and promotion campaigns. When it comes to putting on our own show we seem to fall apart.

Perhaps modesty prevents us from blowing our own horn. Or maybe some of us still regard consulting as a profession and advertising as unprofessional. Or perhaps we just don't understand the techniques of promoting ourselves. Whatever the reason, consultants as a group do a horrible job. This is a shame. An ad campaign for consultants isn't really that difficult, as long as you follow some basic principles.

1. Keep the presentation low-key, conservative, tasteful.

2. Use desk top publishing for most of the work (a real cost-saver and you can be as creative as you wish).

3. Match an advertising campaign to long-range strategic objectives (go after the markets you want to develop).

4. Target specific market niches (stay away from general advertising).

5. Measure results and modify the campaign if not effective.

A good friend from Perreault & Co., Inc., an intermediary consulting firm in Anaheim Hills, California, came up with an advertising scheme that nets the broadest coverage of his niche markets at a minimum cost. He calls it the "rule of 9." He and eight other associated firms operate a network to attract new clients and keep existing ones informed about new developments.

Each member has a fax and when one of the nine comes up with an interesting idea, or sees a new book or article that could be of interest to clients, the network member writes up a one page announcement on the firm's letterhead. This sheet, together with a one page advertising circular for the group, gets faxed to each of the nine members.

All group members then fax the same documents to nine of their close contacts, who do the same to nine more, and on and on. Geometrically, if the pyramid reaches the fifth level, which it usually does, the original document goes out to 59,000 recipients. The group averages a 20 percent achievement rate and that means 11,000 potential new clients get the message! Not bad for the cost of two fax messages each.

Once they get rolling, consultants have proven to be very effective at coming up with creative advertising campaigns. Here are a few advertising media that members of my consortium have used effectively over the years.

1. Direct mail to lawyers, public accountants, financial planners and other business-related professionals
2. Full page newspaper advertisements
3. Highway billboards
4. Television and radio talk shows
5. Television and radio spot commercials
6. Advertisements in trade journals, business magazines, and community affairs bulletins such as school catalogs and community theater playbills

But selecting a medium is only part of the answer. Before running an ad we need to determine what to say. An effective advertisement has four elements:

1. A positive promise of benefit. "Want to save taxes? We'll make it happen." "Looking for financing? We'll arrange it for you." "Need to control your costs? We can do it with computers!"

2. Established performance credentials. "Twenty years in the business." "Over one hundred satisfied clients." "We guarantee to maximize your refund."

3. Proof of credentials. The best proof comes from names and testimonials from satisfied clients.

4. A response mechanism. Telephone number. Return coupon. Questionnaire response.

Impact advertisement accomplishes a specific goal. When writing the copy bear in mind what specific goal you are trying to accomplish. Are you aiming for walk-in business? 10,000 coupon responses? An avalanche of phone calls? Choose only one goal. Target the advertisement to achieve one specific response. Of course, if your advertisement is successful, it helps to be prepared to handle the responses as efficiently and expeditiously as possible.

It's also important to direct your copy to the right audience. If you try to attract M & A clients, do you want large corporations, small businesses, mid-size companies, or individuals? What appeals to one will probably not appeal to the others. I have also found it helpful to remember that I am addressing an audience of one, not one hundred, or one thousand. The advertising copy should be worded to point to one individual or one company, not the masses.

Finally, regardless of the medium chosen, it's crucial to prepare advertising copy to define the specific, unique service you are trying to sell. The more specific you get, the higher the probability of a response. "International consultant experienced in all phases of international work" probably won't bring one reply. "Unique financing sources available for facilities expansion in the European Community" stands a much better chance.

PROTECTIVE MARKETING AND MARKET CONTROL

Consultants seem to shy away from the principal tenet of successful marketing: what I like to call "protective marketing."

Protective marketing means exercising those selling techniques that optimize the mix between billable hours, hourly rates, and selling expenses. Market control, the key to protective marketing, is achieved by concentrating your marketing efforts on those niche markets that best suit your strategic objectives.

When business slows down, the temptation is great to go after any work that nets billable hours, regardless of the type of engagement. This is a deadly practice and gets consultants in all kinds of long-term difficulty, as Jon Klammer, a specialist in M & A work, learned the hard way.

When the credit crunch hit, the M & A market dried up. Jon had trouble booking any new jobs and started soliciting small business start-up clients. Accustomed to Lehman scale fees for M & A work, Jon was shocked to learn that start-up jobs didn't command more than $75 per hour. Nevertheless, he implemented an impact advertising campaign that resulted in more than twenty new clients in less than six months. In short order, Jon's billable hours were fully absorbed.

Out of the blue one of his consortium members asked if he was interested in taking on an M & A assignment in England, at Lehman scale rates, for a client looking for an acquisition in the $50 million range. Fully loaded with small business clients (at $75 an hour) Jon couldn't handle the job and turned it down. Four years later, he was still servicing small business clients and never did get back into M & A work. He is also much poorer for it.

Consultants achieve market control by actions taken in one or a combination of three steps: by optimizing the mix of services performed (don't get over-loaded in one market niche), by focusing on the most lucrative client mix (don't get saddled with slow payers or complainers), and by paying close attention to post-engagement follow-up.

Optimizing service mix means selectively selling those services that optimize billable hours and hourly rates. The most lucrative client mix refers to the solicitation of clients willing and able to pay the highest price for services that you can produce with your talents and organization. Post-engagement follow-up offers the most efficient means of assuring repeat business and glowing references.

Some consultants argue the impracticality of concentrating on marketing those services that yield the highest fees. Doing so would leave vast gaps in available time or reduce gross billings, as in the case of Jon Klammer. There just aren't enough good clients around to be that selective, they say.

Such arguments ring true if consultants continue down the traditional path of servicing market niches that do not offer positive growth potential. As earlier chapters described, traditional organizations, production methods, and marketing tactics preclude market control.

It's impossible to exercise market control if you are merely one of several hundred consultants all offering the same service to the same clients with nothing unique to separate you from the pack. You will never attain market control if you continue to try to be all things to all people. Market control can never be achieved unless you have a special talent that sets you apart, unless you broadcast this talent through effective marketing methods, and unless the talent allows you to specialize in a few of the high growth cutting-edge markets.

SELLING TECHNIQUES

We all have talents and limitations for using different types of selling techniques. Some of us do best with written communications. Others prefer telephone solicitations. Still others work best in face-to-face meetings. Two truisms relate to selling consulting skills to new clients: at least one-third of annual hours should be dedicated to marketing new clients, and the worst mistake anyone can make in the sales arena is to use selling techniques contrary to a person's abilities.

We have already touched on several techniques using written communications—advertising, newsletters, direct mail, and so on. Telephone solicitation and direct meetings also work if you have the sales talent. Both generally start with cold calls, the hardest of any selling technique and frequently the least productive.

Cold Call Selling

I stopped making cold calls several years ago when I finally realized that this was not my forte. On the other hand, a close friend has become expert at using cold calls. He is so successful that it's about the only method he uses any more.

Other consultants have told me that with the right personality cold calls do work. Here are a few tips they have passed along over the years that seem to form the nucleus of successful selling:

1. Plan the call. Before picking up the phone or knocking on a door, know precisely whom to ask for and what your sales pitch will be. When trying to land a strategic planning job it doesn't do much good to speak with the purchasing manager. Once you get through to the right person, you have about thirty seconds to make your pitch. Have three or four sentences prepared that get your message across.

2. Ask for the order. No one has time to chat with a stranger. Keep the conversation short, to the point, and wrap it up with a direct request for an engagement.

3. Target markets. The time has passed for consultants to be hired for general consulting work. Clients now want a specific problem solved. Do enough research to identify which companies are most likely to need your specific service. If you can find out ahead of time, talk to the person responsible for getting the problem solved.

4. Ask for recommendations. If the person you call doesn't want your service, ask for recommendations of managers within the same company or other companies who might need your help. If possible, get the prospect to make an advance telephone call on your behalf.

5. Use indirect leads. Lawyers, public accountants, financial planners, and bank loan officers all have clients/customers with problems. Call on these people for leads.

6. Show concern. Talk about the prospect's personal concerns, banking problems, personnel shortcomings, increased competition, dropping orders, and so on. Be genuine. Show compassion. Convey a sincere desire to help.

7. Do not talk about yourself. Focus attention on the prospect. Stay away from your own interests, unless asked. Then keep the answer short. Let the prospect do the talking. Learn whatever you can in the time allotted.

8. Leave sales literature. Business cards, company brochures, advertising flyers, a newsletter (if you have one), are all reminders that you have called. Structure the literature to provide evidence of your capabilities to handle specific types of engagements.

9. Follow up. This is the most important step. Never, regardless of the reception, allow a prospect to get away with only one call. Always go back a second time, even if turned down cold the first time. Persistence pays.

Hard Sell or Soft Sell

Although not a raging argument, the question of hard versus soft selling tactics continues to arise. Some consultants feel that hard sell tactics are unprofessional. Baloney! Doctors, lawyers, public accountants, dentists, architects, and many other professionals use hard sell tactics consistently. A hard sell is effective if properly structured. As with sales promotions of any kind, if done in good taste, the public views the presentation as professional.

This doesn't mean that consultants should storm the doors of prospective clients, discourteously refusing to take no for an answer. On the contrary, a soft entrance can lead to a dynamic sales pitch. Self-confidence, expert capability, honesty, commitment, all vital consulting characteristics, can be most effectively conveyed through a dynamic, hard-hitting sales pitch—but keep it short.

Persistent follow-up calls are also viewed by some consultants as a poor approach. They feel that a prospect will be embarrassed if continually assaulted with follow-up calls and mailings. Perhaps that's true in some cases. I have found, however, that persistence always pays. Follow-up calls one, two, even three years after the initial contact have consistently yielded clients.

Some people are incapable of projecting a dynamic image and find it difficult, if not impossible to use hard sell tactics. Then they should turn to the soft sell, which can be equally effective in certain markets and with certain clients.

It seems that the larger the client company, the more susceptible representatives are to soft sell techniques. Internal politics play a major role in landing such engagements. Political acumen, indirect referrals, external references all influence the success or failure of a sales call. Hard sell tactics with such prospects nearly always fail to generate anything but headaches.

Using hard sell tactics when your personality exudes conservatism not only backfires, it makes you look silly. Far better to structure marketing campaigns to accentuate your strengths. If this means a slower growth rate or more hours dedicated to marketing, so be it. We can only do what we are capable of doing.

Jumping the "That's the way it's done" Hurdle

When I first became active in the government contracting segment of the aerospace industry I met what seemed to be an immovable obstacle. Well thought-out recommendations fell on deaf ears. Suggestions about solutions used by many companies in other industries were stifled with the statement, "That will never work here. The way we're doing it (the method, procedure, evaluation, negotiation) is the way it's done in the aerospace industry. You can't change it."

The aerospace industry is not alone. Companies the world over use this same excuse against recommended changes. And consultants the world over have two courses to follow: give up and walk away, or jump the hurdle.

Two ways seem to work efficiently in beating this reluctance to change: the client's CEO or other ranking executive can dictate that people will follow your lead, or you can convert client employees by demonstrating the wisdom of your recommendations. Clearly, the latter brings better results for the client. Here's how one consultant beat the odds when engaged to help a mid-size freight hauler develop a strategic planning process.

One of Dick's strategic recommendations was to enter the intermodal freight business. He saw a skyrocketing market for hauling both imports and exports and believed that the company's resources justified the move. The client's vice president of traffic was obstinate, claiming that intermodal freight could never be introduced competitively because it just wasn't the way things were done in that industry. Dick convinced the board to budget $100,000 for a small advertising program to test his case. Within four months calls for intermodal service flooded the client's switchboard. Dick was obviously vindicated.

Engagements limited to solving purely internal problems present a greater challenge. Creative techniques for bringing client employees into the fold seem to work best when they know that implementing your solutions won't jeopardize their job security. A simple statement to this effect from the CEO usually does the trick.

COMBINING FORCES

One of the best ways to augment a consulting organization is by using networks, consortiums, or informal partnerships. Such a combining of forces benefits firms with several partners and staff as well as sole practitioners. It is also a terrific way to get a new business off the ground.

By combining forces consultants offer clients a broader base of skills and more personnel to get the job done rapidly. Combined forces also permits marketing to a broader range of market niches.

In addition to adding to the marketing and production capabilities, combining forces often results in significant overhead and marketing cost savings. A wide variety of overhead expenses can be shaved: office rent, automobile leases and insurance, secretarial and office personnel, office equipment and supplies, telephones, research libraries and data bases, computer software, and many other incidentals.

By combining marketing efforts, not only are a significant amount of selling costs reduced, but the effectiveness of a marketing campaign becomes greatly enhanced. I can hear long-term consultants raise the age-old objection: "I'm not going to let other consultants talk to my clients or even know who they are. They might steal them from me!" We seem to have some proprietary interest in our clients to feel this way. We also must suffer from an intense inferiority complex to believe that client loyalty is so shallow.

Nevertheless, one of the maladies of the consulting business seems to be that most consultants do not talk with one another, much less share marketing information. This is a shame. So many benefits arise from broadening our capabilities that to ignore consortiums, networking, or informal partnerships because we fear losing the clients we have seems like a horrible waste. I have used all three combinations in my consulting lifetime and swear by the results. As a sole practitioner, I could never have built my business in the market niches I wanted without the help of a great number of other consultants.

One huge benefit to sole practitioners of combining forces is the image a larger consulting business presents to a potential client. A united front casts the image of a company as being much bigger than it really is. When competing in a market with larger firms, this can be a crucial protective marketing strategy. A sole practitioner trying to compete with Andersen, BCG, or McKinsey can hardly be expected to control a market niche. The same consultant with the ability to draw from diverse talents of several other consultants stands a much better chance of winning jobs.

An effective impact advertising campaign and well-conceived publicity efforts quickly make the point to the marketplace that you are not alone, a one-man band, with limited resources and work schedules. A comprehensive advertising campaign touting the virtues of the group conveys a strong support organization, varied talents, broad resources, and the ability to handle major engagements. If you try this route it won't take long to realize that this is the only way a sole practitioner can build a profitable business within a reasonable time period.

Other than getting over the hurdle of proprietary clients, two problems seem the most bothersome when sharing advertising or promotion campaigns: deciding on the type of advertising to do, and avoiding conflicts of interest. There is no easy answer to the first problem. You just have to sit down with the group and try to iron out differences. The second problem is easier to deal with. Most conflict of interest situations have to do with how to price each service, how to bill the customer/client, and how to collect.

Informal Partnerships

Informal partnerships seem to be especially popular with sole practitioners, both in the beginning and after they get established. No formal partnership agreement is executed. Partners do not share business liabilities, income, or expenses. No partnership tax returns are filed and no state or federal identification numbers are used. An informal partnership is not a legal entity. Each partner continues to operate as an independent consultant.

The difference from being completely on your own arises when you work on one of your partner's jobs or deal with one of your partner's clients. Then you act under your partner's name, not your own. The client billing goes out on your partner's invoice, not yours. Your partner collects from the client and then reimburses you for work performed.

This sounds more complicated than it is. Informal partnerships proliferate in the consulting industry. Most clients don't realize the partnership is informal. It appears to be a true partnership or an employer/employee relationship. In reality, you sell your services to your partner as an independent contractor. I worked this way when I was between major consulting engagements and had excess billable time.

I now use informal partnerships when I consult to other consultants, which has evolved into a major part of my business. For example, a consultant friend recently needed help sourcing foreign financing for a client. I helped him locate appropriate sources, assisted in developing negotiating strategy, and put the consultant in touch with a competent overseas attorney. The consultant billed my hours and then paid me. I earned income. My partner satisfied his client in a timely manner. Everyone was a winner.

Informal partnerships do not have to be between consultants serving the same markets. Nor are they limited to arrangements between two or more consultants. Informal partnerships work well between consultants and public accountants, investment advisors, financial planners, and certain types of lawyers.

Administratively informal partnerships must stay informal, without legal trappings. Partners must remain free to handle their own businesses. On the other hand, there should be a brief written document spelling out the relationship between the two parties. It should identify how various matters will be shared: billings, occupancy expenses, insurance programs, personnel, getting out positions, and so on. The agreement should be non-binding, however. As soon as two or more independently minded entrepreneurs start trying to use the law to keep a partnership together it inevitably falls apart.

Consortiums

Consortiums offer another popular choice for sharing work loads. A consortium represents a temporary alliance of two or more firms in a common venture. Consortiums work best between consulting firms with different capabilities serving the same market niches. Small firms specializing in international assignments or those concentrating on extended engagement turnaround clients rely heavily on consortiums to fill in the skill gaps.

The production side of these engagements demands such a diverse mix of specialized skills, personal contacts, and management acumen that seldom does a sole practitioner, or a small firm, have access to all these resources. The solution is to call on a consortium of consultants offering a breadth of capabilities and contacts.

A good example of how consulting consortiums work in troubled company engagements occurred recently. A sole practitioner took on an extended turnaround engagement that required him to assume a general management role at the client's location for six months. A number of issues needed resolution during this period—refinancing, tax planning, personnel recruiting, computer systems installation, the divestiture of a subsidiary, and the acquisition of a distribution company. Obviously, a single consultant can't be expert in all these areas. The consultant called on consortium members to help with the M & A work, tax planning, and refinancing, while he handled the balance of the work.

Each consulting firm maintained its own identity and billed the client separately, although the billing could easily have been consolidated in one invoice from the original sole practitioner. The billing practice depends entirely on client preference.

Consortiums are a terrific way to increase billings, and hence cash flow, with a minimal marketing effort. Consortiums also represent one of the fastest ways to develop a public image as a quality company capable of handling large jobs as well as small.

As a temporary alliance, consortiums can be formed without any formal agreement or legally binding contract. It's just a matter of searching out consultants who augment your specialty and informally agreeing to sell and perform complementary services together.

Networking

Networking is very similar to consortiums except that the identification of each of the firms included in the network is not used as a marketing tool. Frequently non-consulting firms, lawyers, financial planners, tax advisors, computer and other specialists network with consultants. Only the diverse capabilities of each specialty are marketed. And each member markets the skills of all other participants. The basic idea in networking is to offer clients a complete service capability that crosses many disciplines without incurring payroll costs or the complexities of a partnership.

Since each network participant advertises full service capability, when a job is landed calling for skills not resident in the member booking the order, one of the other specialists is called upon to perform the work. The customer can either be billed by each company performing work or by the firm booking the order, who then pays each participant.

Consulting firms serving a large regional or national market use networking to share the work load in different parts of the country, thus reducing or eliminating travel expenses. In this case, networking becomes a referral service and the business booking the order gets a referral fee. Regardless of which format is used, sharing work loads permits consulting firms to increase billings and serve larger markets than they could possibly do individually.

Networking, consortiums, or informal partnerships enable consultants to attract much larger engagements, market to a broader base of potential clients, and diversify into a wider range of market niches, without the implicit or explicit constraints of formal business combinations. New consultants learn quickly that any one of these methods increases the likelihood of building a successful business.

5 Project-Oriented Markets

Project engagements have a beginning and an end. Their success or failure is easily measured by both the client and the consultant. Most tend to be one-shot assignments; once the project is completed the client seldom wants the same work repeated. Larger companies remain the exception. With several manufacturing locations, for example, a client might want a similar computer system installed in each location. Certain types of projects, such as M & A engagements, won't foster repeat business immediately, but conceivably in two to three years the client might want to make another acquisition or divestiture.

Some projects have a higher likelihood of repeat business than others. A consulting firm might be called back to recruit management personnel whenever the client needs a new body. Market studies for different product lines or different customer mixes could repeat as new products or customers are added, or when entirely new markets need to be researched, as in an export business. Conversely, the probability of being called back to perform a second environmental compliance study seems remote.

Management consultants have been handling project assignments for as long as the industry has existed. Many consulting firms build their entire business on one type of project, such as systems installations or personnel recruiting. Many types of project work remain in high demand. Others have faded from view.

The complexity of traditional project work is changing rapidly, however. We might remain committed to systems work, but new market niches have shifted to PCs and associated software and away from mainframe programming and systems design. Consulting firms all over the country know that the demand for project work continues. They are also learning that the types of projects in demand have radically changed over the past four years and will change even more in the future. If they don't learn the new skills and techniques needed to perform these projects clients will become increasingly scarce.

This chapter looks at five types of project engagements that offer the greatest opportunities for getting and keeping clients over the next decade and for charging the highest fees, both now and in the future. The five are:

1. Design and implementation of telecommunications and network PC systems

2. Acquisition, divestiture, and merger work for small and mid-size companies

3. Personnel evaluation and selection

4. New market research and evaluation

5. Environmental compliance

SYSTEMS PROJECTS

Old-time systems consultants cut their teeth on integrated manufacturing systems that depended on mainframe computers. IBM's Production and Inventory Control System (PICS) that later developed the MAPICS and COPICS acronyms was a popular program configuration that integrated order entry, purchasing, inventory control, sales, and accounting software modules into one gigantic system. Clients flocked to the doors of consultants with the ability to design integrated systems that could utilize these programs. For twenty years, mainframe systems projects remained the life blood of consultants as they designed and installed them for all sizes of manufacturing, distribution, and retail clients.

Then microcomputer technology changed computer speeds, sizes, storage capability, and cost. Communications technology gave us access to the world in split second timing. New manufacturing and distribution techniques made PICS and other popular integrated systems outdated. A new breed of computer manufacturers, software developers, and systems programmers pushed companies to accumulate, analyze, and store data in revolutionary ways. Their technology now allows companies to communicate across great distances and to analyze masses of market, product, and competitor information collected from data bases.

Even more important than changes in technology and improved management techniques has been the transfer of responsibility for designing and implementing business systems from professional systems analysts and programmers to the customers who use these systems. Companies have two paths to follow. They can staff internal personnel with the technical ability to do systems work, as most of the large corporations did, or they can engage outside consultants to design and implement new systems. Most smaller and mid-size companies choose the latter route.

As systems technology continues to enhance hardware and software performance an increasing number of operating companies need consulting expertise to make these innovations useful. This, in turn, opens the door for consultants to enter several rapidly growing, specialized project niches for designing and implementing production, distribution, accounting, and analytic systems. Two of the hottest niches over the next decade will be those employing local and remote computer networks, and telecommunication data transfer.

Size and Types of Clients

Businesses of all sizes and shapes employ network systems and telecommunications techniques. Frequently the two go together. Retail establishments, hotels, financial services companies (including banks), distributors, and manufacturers use network systems to cut the cost of stand-alone computers and to provide access to a central bank of information for multiple users. Companies with more than one location integrate high-speed data transmission and distribution techniques with network operating systems.

Telecommunications systems integrated with those of customers and suppliers enables the immediate placement of orders, order confirmations, and payment. Integrating with federal systems automatically records customs, tax, and other compliance reports and payments. As companies enter the international arena, their need increases to transmit accurate and timely data to and from operating divisions, customers, suppliers, and government agencies located in far-flung global locations.

Although most companies currently using networks and sophisticated telecommunication techniques are mid-size or large corporations, an increasing number of smaller companies in all industries are finding that competition forces them to join the fray. It seems safe to say that in the years ahead practically every business of any size will use microcomputers with either network or telecommunications capabilities, or both.

Qualifications, Certification, Experience

To date, no federal or state law requires consultants to be licensed or certified to perform systems work. This could change, however, as government becomes increasingly involved in controlling private enterprise. On the other hand, special skills are necessary to establish credentials.

As a minimum, consultants should have hard-core experience in both the use and the installation of network and/or telecommunications software. Ideally, this experience would come from previous employment or from performing peripheral consulting work for clients concurrently installing these systems. Software and hardware manufacturers also offer indoctrination courses for both technicians and users.

Many hardware and software retail outlets do a good job of training users, although technical expertise is often lacking. Universities and trade schools also offer both technical and user courses. Some trade groups have recognized the large number of member companies that are unsophisticated in computer applications and offer training seminars and conferences. A limited number of SBA offices staff personnel qualified to teach such courses.

Although programming capability is certainly a plus, consultants without such training can easily pick up enough to handle most client needs. With a little effort, most consultants who have the aptitude and desire to get into this market should have no difficulty learning or brushing up on required skills.

Organization

Nearly all systems projects must be performed on the client's premises. Depending on the complexity of the installation, consultants might be away from their office for one week, one month, or several months. Periods arise during the preliminary stages of an engagement when you can pull off the job for a day or two for other activities. Once the project starts rolling, however, it requires constant attention.

Not only must the technical system work properly but client personnel must be trained to use it. These matters take dedicated time and leave no room for other activities such as marketing efforts, administrative chores, or other engagements. In addition, most systems projects require a crash program to get the systems up and running as soon as possible. Technicians might have to be called in for electrical wiring, program testing, or special hardware hook-ups.

Rarely can a sole practitioner do a satisfactory systems implementation job without help. Consequently, most consultants specializing in this market find that at least one or two other consultants and possibly administrative assistance must be utilized. Organizationally, systems projects work much better for firms of two or three partners than for solo consultants.

This doesn't mean that sole practitioners cannot specialize in this market. On the contrary, many are very successful. They cover themselves by utilizing network or consortium affiliates. A prime example occurred when Maxine left Laventhol & Horwath and started her own firm to help ex-Laventhol clients install network systems. Her first engagement involved the installation of a local network in a 300-room hotel and a telecommunications hook-up with four other hotel and offices located from New York to Washington, DC.

Maxine called in two consortium consultants to help install the systems in the client's remote locations while she managed the local network implementation. The first user application was the accounting system, which Maxine handled. She brought in another hotel specialist to implement the front desk system. As a footnote, the success of this job brought Maxine three more clients in rapid succession. She used consortium members on all engagements.

Fee Structure

Although some consultants persist in sticking with an hourly billing practice, most clients prefer a flat, not-to-exceed fee for the entire project. With a not-to-exceed fee, consultants must be careful to specify that follow-up work will be billed at additional hourly rates. Too often, systems implementation projects need revisions, changes, user instruction, and a variety of other work that you cannot charge for without a follow-up hourly rate agreement. It doesn't take many hours to eat up profits from the installation phase.

Repeat/Continuing Business

Follow-on systems work is rare. Clients seldom want to put up with work flow disruptions a second time. Generally, if they want more than one system they contract for it at the initial engagement. Occasionally, follow-on systems work arises, but when it does it's usually with larger companies for installations in remote locations. Once the system gets running efficiently, continuing consultation work is usually a lost cause.

Getting Clients

Several avenues exist for soliciting systems clients. Referrals from public accounting firms or from ex-employers are two of the best. Public accountants always look for better ways to ensure efficient accounting and internal control in client companies. Some public accountants try to do the systems work themselves. Most fail badly. The smart ones keep one or two consulting firms in their files to call upon when the need arises.

Ex-employers are another good source. In the previous example, Maxine landed her first engagement from a client of her ex-employer, Laventhol & Horwath.

Referrals from retail computer hardware and software dealers can also be a source of new clients. Smaller companies particularly expect retailers to help with the system implementation. However, very few dealers are either qualified or want to do this. Most larger dealers maintain tickler files of systems consultants qualified to handle the engagement.

Software manufacturers are another good source of referrals, especially if you also act as a dealer for their software. Some consultants have developed a second source of income by selling software to clients as well as installing it (quite common with accounting software). Manufacturers then refer prospective customers to the dealer, who reaps a profit on the software sale as well as the installation.

Direct marketing methods can also be effective. Advertisements in computer magazines bring in a modest number of clients. Participation in industry trade shows is more effective. Although costly, a small booth advertising your systems capability can work wonders. Use registration cards to solicit responses.

ACQUISITION, DIVESTITURES, AND MERGERS

The M & A business is alive and well, contrary to media reports. And indications abound that it will pick up significant momentum in the years ahead. Ex-executives continue to provide a major pool of buyers. Corporations of varying sizes continue to dispose of divisions and subsidiaries and pick up new ones. Like other consulting markets, however, the character of the M & A niche is changing rapidly, requiring new skill and marketing directions.

Globalization causes companies to look at overseas acquisitions as a quick entry to new markets. The onslaught of corporate executives thrown on the streets, some with, some without golden parachute cash, seek acquisition opportunities of small, rapid growth companies. Owners of companies facing troubled times try to dump their holdings before the company goes under. Corporate giants languishing in stable or declining product lines look for acquisitions in diverse markets to bring new life to their P/E ratio. Couple this demand with radically shifting financing sources, and qualified consultants should have more work than they can handle for years to come.

Engagement Characteristics

Assistance for buyers requires a different set of production efforts than helping sellers. In the former case, buyers need varying degrees of help in seven areas:

- Locating target candidates
- Valuing the target company
- Negotiating price and terms
- Structuring a due diligence program
- Arranging financing
- Coordinating with legal counsel
- Closing

Divestiture or selling engagements involve less work:

- Locating potential buyers
- Valuing the company
- Negotiating assistance
- Closing

Obviously, the degree to which each of these steps is needed depends upon the sophistication and resources of buyers and sellers.

Client Size

To establish a broad enough base, consultants should stay away from large corporate buyers and sellers. It's difficult to penetrate the latter. They usually turn to comparably large investment banks to assist in selling a large division or subsidiary. The same problem exists when trying to attract giant buyers. Once the board decides to acquire, an investment bank, corporate legal counsel, in-house acquisition staffs, and financial analysts all get into the act.

It seems senseless to compete at this level when the market consists of so many other potential clients. The best policy calls for targeting ex-executives and mid-size companies for buyers, and small or mid-size companies for sellers. On the other hand, the dismal record of many large corporate acquisition staffs foretells increasing reliance on outside help, at least as far as sourcing targets. Perhaps a market will develop there as well.

Qualifications, certification, experience

M & A work does not require certification or licensing. It does require hands-on experience with either an acquisition or a divestiture. During the past ten years literally thousands of unqualified business brokers have come out of the woodwork trying to convince selling companies to list with them, just like with a real estate agent. They also pester buyers to contract with them for acquisition searches. Very, very few of these brokers know what they are doing. Thousands of both buyers and sellers have been stung.

This intrusion has driven many qualified M & A consultants into other specialties. Although qualified competition has lessened as a result, M & A consulting has received a black eye. It doesn't take long for a client to spot incompetence. If you can't offer at least some background in acquisitions or divestitures to substantiate your credentials, don't try to penetrate this field alone. Learn the ropes first by teaming up with an experienced M & A consultant from your consortium.

Organization

One of the real benefits of M & A consulting is that a good part of the work load can be done from your office. Occasional travel to the site of target candidates, research libraries, or financing sources is necessary, but most of the work can be done by phone.

Data bases abound that can be tapped for target leads. Target referrals from consortium or network members come by phone or by fax. Analyses of company financial statements for valuation purposes can be done in your office. Even financial institutions can be sourced by phone or fax.

With their office as the prime production site, sole practitioners find M & A consulting a terrific niche market. They can make time for marketing and administration and avoid large segments of nonproductive travel time. Tying into a national consulting network solves most of the problems associated with target and finance sourcing. Of course when it's time to negotiate and then close the deal, clients frequently want their own consultant to hold their hand. But these steps only take a few days away from the office.

A good rule of thumb in M & A work is not to take on more than three engagements at one time. In a normal month of 168 available hours, using the 60-40 rule allows 60 percent of 168 or 100 hours for production. With three clients, each gets about thirty-three hours per month. Without travel time, thirty to forty hours per month serves the client well over a six to nine month engagement. And it leaves plenty of time for marketing and administration.

Fee Structures

Although consultants become very creative when billing M & A work, the old Lehman scale remains a good standard:

5 percent for the first million dollars of selling price

4 percent for the next million

3 percent for the next

2 percent for the next

1 percent for the next

1/2 percent for the excess over $5 million

Experienced M & A consultants insist on monthly retainers equal to the amount of time they plan to commit the following month. A common range for smaller clients is $4,000 to $5,000, for thirty-three hours. Retainers for larger, corporate clients range upwords from $20,000.

Although sometimes hard to sell, a monthly retainer is absolutely necessary. Too many deals die half way through the process, or even at the very end, after you put in six to nine months of effort. Since the typical closing fee based on the Lehman scale, or otherwise, is contingent upon closing, it's very easy to lose substantial billings without a retainer. Some consultants apply the retainer against the closing fee. Others charge retainers in addition to it.

Geographic Boundaries

Successful M & A consultants do not put arbitrary boundaries on their engagements. Since most production work emanates from the office, it doesn't make much difference if the buyer, seller, and consultant are thousands of miles apart.

Marketing

A few consultants have successfully marketed their services through advertisements in trade journals or other publications. Most frown on advertising, however, believing it puts them in the same sleazy category as unscrupulous business brokers.

Most good clients come through referrals. Although lawyers specializing in acquisition work and a few of the larger public accountant firms can at times be helpful, the best referrals come through financial institutions. Large commercial banks, foreign banks, investment banks, and venture capital firms, are all excellent sources of leads to both buyer and seller clients.

One of the first steps for anyone seriously interested in getting into M & A consulting should be an intensive publicity program aimed at getting introductions to financial organizations. Cold calls and direct mailings hardly ever work here. Once again, the "business broker" image.

Write a book about acquisitions and divestitures. Speak to groups of potential buyers, sellers, and bankers. Submit articles on the subject to trade journals, major banks, and small venture capital and investment banking groups. Each of these methods brings in clients.

Post-Closing Follow-Up

The mark of successful M & A consultants is that they care about the results of the acquisition or divestiture after closing. Buyers need all the help they can get learning the ropes of the new company and assimilating it into their organization. Very frequently, a follow-up call at this point brings additional engagements in other, non-M & A work. Sellers also need consoling after the deal closes. Corporate sellers not infrequently bring the same M & A consultant in for the next divestiture or to assist with other problems.

PERSONNEL EVALUATION AND SELECTION PROJECTS

From the ashes of traditional management recruiting engagements a new consulting specialty has been born. Revolutionary changes in global business and increased management specialization in high tech disciplines have brought a wealth of business to professional recruiters and executive search firms. Many do an excellent job ferreting out lists of candidates from chairman of the board to vice president of sales. Without a detailed knowledge of the client's operating conditions, management style, or long-range objectives, however, these recruiters cannot go beyond recommending several candidates. The final evaluation and selection process must be left to the client, even though search fees for this half-job have gone through the roof, exceeding a new hire's annual salary.

Client personnel, ill-equipped to evaluate either an applicant's highly specialized technical ability or, in many cases, how the applicant matches up with the company's specific objectives, leave the door open to very costly and time-consuming errors. Enter management consultants, fully knowledgeable about client personnel, management style, technical needs, and objectives. With no axe to grind, consultants usually do a far superior job evaluating top management candidates than either search firms or clients.

The market for these services typically centers on smaller or mid-size companies trying to recruit new management for a critical change in the company's objectives—such as embarking on an important acquisition expansion drive, a major move to new markets, or establishing an overseas facility. Although recruiting engagements normally come as follow-ons to previous consulting assignments, with increasing frequency companies are searching out specialists to handle the evaluation segment exclusively. This is especially true for recruiting overseas managers.

Qualifications and Experience

Although a background in human relations disciplines can be helpful it certainly is not necessary. Anyone who has recruited managers or has been on the receiving end knows what questions to ask. Besides, the executive search firm has already asked 90 percent of them. By the time you meet the candidate only three aspects need to be evaluated:

- Do the candidate's personality and personal work standards match those of top client personnel?

- Do the candidate's work habits complement those of managers with whom the candidate will be in close contact?
- Is the candidate technically capable of performing the job the client needs done?

If you know client personnel well enough, if you have technical expertise in the same discipline as the candidate, and if you have performed the same or a similar job as the candidate is seeking, you shouldn't need any other qualifications.

Organization

No organization problems arise in this niche unless you perform evaluation interviews in distant locations, such as overseas. Usually, however, the applicant can be brought to either your office or the client's office.

Fee Structures

If the engagement is not a follow-on to an existing or prior assignment, fees for recruiting work are normally set at a flat rate. Although significantly less than what an executive search firm charges, the fee should relate to the value the client places on filling the slot. If the client is looking for a new CEO the fee can be much higher than if you interview candidates for vice president.

If several positions need to be filled, or if several candidates must be evaluated, a monthly retainer fee should be negotiated. When and if the client hires the candidate, this retainer can be applied against the evaluation fee. If the engagement is a follow-on to previous or current work, then obviously your normal billing rate should be used.

Marketing

It's nearly impossible to advertise for clients in this specialty, at least within the United States. Executive search and outplacement firms begin the recruiting process so they have the advertising media pretty much to themselves. Consultants come in after the search firms finish.

Therefore, the best source of clients should be referrals from these same search firms.

Executive search firms are not usually very cooperative, however. They pitch the complete job to clients, from start to finish, and this is reflected in the exorbitant fees they charge. Outplacement firms operate differently. They get paid by the client whether an executive gets placed or not. As a means of building their own client base, these firms frequently look for outside help in placing executives. A good word or two to hiring companies can get you in the door faster than any other means.

Overseas personnel selection is a different story. Whereas search firms actively solicit foreign business from American clients, they don't have the market sewed up. Soliciting referrals from overseas offices of "Big Six" public accounting firms, from branches of American banks, and from local trade groups can build a client base in no time.

Repeat Business/Client Referrals

Once you start handling management evaluation and selection projects, both repeat business and client referrals seem to flow fairly regularly. As long as the demand for executive specialists exceeds the supply, clients will continue to call on management consultants who can deliver the goods.

NEW MARKET RESEARCH AND EVALUATION PROJECTS

Market research projects lead to all types of varying assignments. As a way to broaden a client base, this niche can't be beaten. A few of the projects that fall into this market are to:

- Determine market size, competition, and pricing structure for client's new product introductions.
- Evaluate market demand for a new technology being developed by client.
- Identify government, industry, and market implicit and explicit barriers to expanding client product lines.

- Test effectiveness of advertising campaign.
- Establish market control criteria for client niches.
- Assist client in identifying and structuring protective marketing tactics.
- Identify competitors' potential new product introductions and impact on market.
- Restructure client cost estimating and pricing procedures.

Clearly, these represent a limited number of examples. Clients have varying needs for information and analyses of market reaction to new products, technologies, competition, pricing structures, product line profitability, and customer mix.

The end result of a market/product evaluation project might take the form of a comprehensive report identifying methods used and conclusions. More likely, the final product is a financial forecast, by product line or market, that identifies the most likely outcome of taking recommended actions, presumably resulting in increased sales, profitability, return on investment, and cash flow.

Not infrequently, this type of engagement leads to an extended assignment assisting the client to develop a two or three-year operating plan or even a long-term strategic plan.

Client Size

Although companies of virtually every size need help in market and product evaluation, smaller ones generally either can't afford to hire a consultant or don't recognize their need for outside guidance. Engagements usually come from mid-size or larger clients with several product lines or serving several markets. Many have R & D programs. Most sport forward-thinking top managers already moving toward programs to increase market share or improve product line profitability. If they aren't already moving along this path clients are unlikely to pay the higher fees these engagements command.

Fee Structure

Market research and evaluation projects typically get billed at hourly rates. It is difficult to estimate how long the project will take until you actually begin; therefore, flat fees are impractical. Some consultants work off monthly retainers, especially when the client is new or unknown to the consultant. Generally, however, the size and type of client willing to pay for this service can be relied upon to pay after the fact. Except for M & A work, hourly rates for these projects run higher than most others, typically 20 to 30 percent higher.

Organization

The length of market research engagements runs all over the lot. Some are very simple and can be completed in two or three days. Others take months to bring to fruition. A few require start and stop activities over an extended period. Such variations make it extremely difficult for solo practitioners to make a major mark in this niche. The unpredictability of billable hours leaves too wide a gap in planned marketing activities.

Most of the engagements fall to firms with at least two partners. Informal partnerships also work. More often than not, these projects complement other market niches to round out a client base.

Networking and consortiums don't seem to help much. The nature of the work frequently makes it a one-person job with only slight variations in skills. In most cases specialized expertise provided by network or consortium members does not add to production capability.

Marketing

Most consultants attract market research clients because of specialized industry, technical, or regional expertise. Clients that want evaluations of new market or product potentials in the Caribbean look to consultants with expertise in doing business in the Caribbean. A company trying to introduce a diet-aid drug wants a consultant with background in the pharmaceutical industry. Market testing a new filter to eliminate toxic fumes requires a knowledge of EPA regulations.

Impact advertising campaigns and publicity shots extolling a consultant's credentials in such specialty fields bring good results. So do references from ex-employers or ex-clients in these markets. Active participation in related trade association functions also attracts clients. One or all of these passive sales techniques should bring in enough work to make a mark.

Of all the marketing techniques, cold calls seem to be the least effective. The "this is the way it's done in this industry" syndrome effectively precludes active selling. Better to stick with the passive techniques.

Repeat Business

Of all the hot project-type market niches, market and product evaluation engagements provide the greatest opportunity for repeat business. Repeat engagements come either from additional evaluation projects or from expansion into other types of assignments.

While participating in the Philadelphia Boat Show, the CEO of a small boat accessories manufacturer asked me to handle the market evaluation of four new products he planned to introduce over the following year. I must have completed the project to his satisfaction because within two months I was back in his plant installing a computer-based cost system.

A two-partner consulting firm from Detroit focused on market and product evaluation projects for new materials technology used in the automobile industry. The firm received several repeat engagements from a base of four clients. Three years later, these same four clients continue to represent 90 percent of the firm's annual billings.

ENVIRONMENTAL COMPLIANCE ENGAGEMENTS

Increasingly restrictive state and federal environmental protection laws foretell an escalating need for consulting expertise in this area. Industrial contaminants continue to pollute the air, water, ground, and food supply. In most cases, the enormous cost of converting to fuel-efficient, pollutant-free processes prohibits manufacturers from voluntarily complying with stringent EPA regulations.

Four conditions are beginning to impact the approach companies take to safeguard the environment:

- Stiff fines from state and federal environmental agencies
- Recognition of third-party liability by lenders and investors

- Accelerating pressure from consumer groups
- Increased competition from socially responsible companies

Consultants enter the environmental picture from three vantage points. Client engagements involve:

1. Evaluating compliance with federal and state EPA regulations and determining potential liability
2. Recommending solutions for cleaning up previously contaminated areas
3. Proposing and evaluating alternative methods to prevent future contamination

The increasing number of foreign companies that have set up shop in the United States but remain unfamiliar with compliance requirements has created one group of prospective clients for environmental consultants. The ruralization of manufacturing companies to previously uncontaminated areas creates another. Aging urban companies make up a third. Stricter interpretations of lender liability laws force banks to obtain independent compliance opinions prior to granting loans or loan extensions, creating yet another potential client group. And on it goes. Potential clients for environmental consultants seem limitless. There can be little doubt that this market niche will continue to explode for years to come.

Qualifications, Certification, Experience

To date, environmental consultants do not have to be certified or licensed. It helps, however, to obtain certification in a related engineering discipline. It is highly probable that in the future, some type of state or federal licensing or proof of expertise will be mandated. Experiential credentials, however, are definitely required now.

Most of us do not have such credentials, which is one reason so little competition exists in this new niche market. And most of us have no intention of going back to school to become environmental engineers. Networking provides the solution.

Environmental consulting can be used as an entry to other engagements. And, conversely, other engagements breed environmental work. Let the environmental engineers handle the technical part through a networking association. Bring them in as sub-contractors, or as independent consultants. Either way, your client relationship remains intact because it will be up to you to translate the environmentalist's recommendations into usable solutions for the client.

Organization

The technical aspect of this type of consulting engagement is relatively short-lived. Surveys of client facilities and field investigations take days, not weeks. Time away from the office is minor. Report writing, analysis, and research can all be done from the office. On the other hand, it's hard to tell in the beginning what type of work will evolve from an environmental assignment. Conceivably it could branch out into significant on-site project work. Networking takes care of the technical side and alleviates any need for special organization considerations.

Although a few have started their own environmental consulting businesses, most environmental engineers remain employed by engineering firms. Many of these employees moonlight in the evening and weekends and provide an excellent source of networking talent.

Marketing

Several advertising and public relations programs work well for attracting environmental clients. Impact advertisements in trade journals, newspapers, and business magazines work very well. Public relations campaigns involving participation in trade seminars and conferences, community and industry presentations, even writing a book portray expertise in the field.

At least for the present, management consultants have left this market to testing labs and large environmental companies such as Roy Weston, Inc., whose main thrust is toward corporate giants. But small and mid-size clients hesitate to go this route mainly because of anticipated high fees. This leaves the door wide open to smaller consulting firms to use this niche for bringing in other business.

Direct selling methods also work. Banks are beginning to recognize their legal liability when lending to customers in default of federal or state environmental regulations. A consulting firm in our consortium recognized this shift. The firm specialized in workout engagements for banks but had access to environmental engineering expertise through the network. When the partners called on bank officials who handled problem loans, they used their environmental compliance capability as a sales promotion gimmick to land workout jobs. They found several banks that eagerly directed their loan customers to the consulting firm for an environmental compliance survey as a prerequisite for a loan renewal or new funding. Once in the door, the consultants pushed for a workout engagement. By the way, always sub-contract the technical environmental work since no one in the firm has the expertise.

Fee Structure

Environmental projects are normally billed in two increments. The first is a flat fee for a survey of the client's facilities and an evaluation report. The second increment involves recommending and, in many cases, implementing solutions. This work is nearly always billed at an hourly rate. Environmental work tends to command fees about 10 percent higher than non-technical project engagements.

These five project niches certainly do not represent all of the categories consultants handle. They do not represent even a small fraction of project engagements traditionally performed. But they are all specialty niche markets that offer substantial opportunities for rapid growth over the next decade.

Few of us have the capability to solicit and produce in all of these markets. But all of us probably have the talent or access to skills outside our business to compete effectively. Technical skills are not the primary concern. The key to project consulting is to have the personal characteristics and organization that fit project work. Either the wrong organization or the wrong mix of personal capabilities and work habits makes project engagements unworkable and, in many cases, unbearable.

6 General Management Markets

General management consulting takes on an entirely different flavor from project work. Organization, fee structure, marketing, and production coordination focus on unstructured work assignments extending for indefinite periods. Specific capabilities and personal work habits must be oriented toward the demands of client senior executives. Finely honed communications talents must focus on a client's internal group dynamics.

Although consultants have been selling general management advice for generations, revolutionary changes in company ownership, control, relationships, and values are now accelerating the demand for new approaches to some very traditional activities. Three top management activities in the greatest need of fresh techniques are strategic planning, organizational development, and employee motivation.

Concurrent with the globalization of markets and resources, companies are shifting their emphasis from short-term earnings maximization to long-term market control. Cross-border ownership structures and global financing sources reduce their dependence on traditional capital markets.

Extended government controls over everything from personnel practices to customer definition overlay independent business decisions. Increased employee ownership and profit-sharing sever traditional relationships between companies and their employees.

Public awareness of the social responsibility of private enterprise shifts top management attention from company growth to influencing public policies and rebukes traditional emphasis on continually increasing shareholder earnings. Instant, transglobal communications and mountains of accessible information prevent managements from hiding behind the cloak of ignorance.

CHANGES IN OWNERSHIP

Traditional theories that point to individual shareholders as the ultimate owners of corporations—entitled to detailed disclosures of company actions and plans and deserving of quarterly dividend checks as a return on their investment—are fading from view. Boards of directors and top management personnel are no longer obligated to emphasize shareholders' return as their ultimate goal.

Board members retain their directorships and top management their positions by satisfying three groups of power brokers: the very limited number of shareholders, predominantly institutions, owning large blocks of common stock; wealthy foreign investors donating capital to keep the company alive; financial institutions controlling the purse strings of the company; and the public at large demanding safer, cleaner and more socially responsible operating policies.

Even though these four groups may not be controlling "owners" in the legal sense, their influence overshadows anything individual shareholders can muster. The leaders of General Motors, Citicorp, Boeing, Procter & Gamble, Johnson & Johnson, and other major corporations are not measured by the dividends they pay shareholders but by how adroitly they manage their affairs to satisfy these four power groups. As in every phase of business, conditions that affect the giant corporations eventually filter down to their smaller cousins.

Global Privatization

Important changes in the ownership structures of corporations throughout the world cast a new light on competitive position and company objectives. They also provide consultants a way to turn traditional general management engagements into new markets demanding new techniques.

British, French, German, Polish, Hungarian, Italian, and many other national governments have embarked on massive privatization programs. This divesting of government-owned companies and entire industries throws large, profit-oriented competitors into the ring.

When owned by governments, these industrial and financial giants did not concern themselves with profits and growth. Now, forced to stand on their own, they must compete in market economies like everyone else. Consultants stand ready to offer strategic and organizational assistance.

With enormous personnel and financial resources at their command, newly privatized companies offer fiercely competitive price and delivery standards for both large and small competitors. This opens a related consulting market with smaller companies facing this new, intense competition.

For a variety of reasons, not the least of which is to prevent takeovers, companies are buying back their stock from the public market. No longer concerned with manipulating short-term share prices these companies have the ability to re-orient corporate objectives to meet long-term goals. New approaches to organization and reporting criteria are desperately needed to implement this changed focus. Employee incentive programs formerly tied to publicly traded stock no longer work. Creative consultants can assist top management move through the transition period as well as aid in the design and implementation of employee motivation policies.

Foreign Ownership

Cross-border ownership shifts corporate objectives to utilize vast sums of international money, materials, management talent, and technology. Competitive goals stretch to global markets. Market control assumes greater importance than immediate earnings growth. Political objectives of both foreign and domestic governments must be fulfilled.

Even large financial institutions are becoming globally owned. Japanese investors own a large chunk of Goldman Sachs; the Swiss took over Bank of Boston; Saudi investors own a significant piece of Citicorp; Banco de Santander of Spain owns 15 percent of First Fidelity Bank; Hong Kong and Shanghai Bank owns Marine Midland.

Executives of companies either controlled or partially owned by foreign partners or investors find that new owners from different cultures expect approaches to long-term planning and organization structure at variance with traditional procedures. Frequently, management personnel become fearful or disgruntled with foreign ownership. Consultants have the ability to assist in restructuring the organization, developing creative motivational programs, and assisting executives meet the long-term challenges of their new owners.

Employee Ownership

The management buyout craze of the 1980s has left many large and small companies in the hands of employees and their related institutions (e.g., pension funds and ESOPs). This means that without fear of losing their jobs, managers can concentrate on maximizing compensation and employee benefits. It also means that the financial institutions that provided the buyout financing now exert a major influence over the company's growth, market share, and cash flow objectives.

Independent consultants can perform a liaison service, co-ordinating communications between financial institutions and management. They can also help management implement strategic and organizational policies to meet the requirements of these financiers.

Government Ownership

The federal government is also getting into the act. Intent on preserving jobs and protecting individual investors, federal agencies such as the Resolution Trust Corp. and the FDIC assume ownership control and install new management to operate banks, hotels, manufacturing companies, and retailers. Rather than focusing on long-term growth objectives, the mission of these new owners is to recoup their investment as soon as possible. Many times this leads to auction price sales of real property, banks, and companies.

Managers remaining from the previous ownership structure must shift gears to direct their objectives to the will of the federal agency. Traditional organization structures often cannot function in this environment. New managers from the federal agencies with little knowledge of the company's peculiar problems and history tend to blunder into massive policy errors.

Consultants can smooth the way for managers from both camps. They can also assist in the disposition of company assets or in the sale of the company in total. They can implement incentive programs to motivate managers, making the switch in operating policies more palatable. They can assist in developing a financially oriented strategic plan to save the company.

Financial Institution Ownership

The federal government isn't the only creditor forcing foreclosure. Banks and other financial institutions, fearful of their own security, opt for foreclosure rather than continued lending. One result is the sale of a company's assets and full liquidation of the business to satisfy outstanding loans. Consultants can assist in the close-down and liquidation proceedings or they can help the creditor operate the company until it becomes profitable and salable.

Most of these financial institutions do not have the management talent to run an operating company. They need all the help they can get to keep qualified managers on board and to implement operating procedures to salvage the company. Consultants fill the gap and many times end up with long-term management engagements either running the company or managing specific functions.

CHANGES IN CONTROL

Along with these revolutionary changes in ownership come equally radical shifts in control measures. Traditionally, senior executives exercised complete control over the fortunes of the company. They controlled the organization structure, personnel policies, choice of product, customer, and market mix, the company's capital structure, and expansion or contraction moves. The CEO and the board of directors in publicly held corporations, or the business owner in privately held companies, exercised complete autonomy in setting policies, implementing procedures, and directing every aspect of the company, including the payment or non-payment of dividends to shareholders/investors.

Three conditions have changed this control pattern and in turn have opened the door to new consulting opportunities: ownership changes previously discussed, restrictive state and federal regulations, and dependence on debt.

Control Exercised by New Owners

When a foreign company acquires controlling ownership new reporting procedures are usually required. Formats of financial statements and other reports are totally different in every country of the world. Consultants who are knowledgeable about the accounting conventions applicable to an acquired client can frequently use this expertise as a way to get in the door.

"Employees"

Employees who take over a company through a management buyout frequently look at internal control procedures differently than their predecessors. Vivid recollections of onerous approval chains, personnel evaluation policies, top management idiosyncrasies, and wasteful separation of duties often lead to an abandonment of many fundamental rules of sound internal control. After a management buyout, control mechanisms seem to fall apart while the new managers/owners search for alternatives.

Enter the consultant. Establishing basic internal controls over cash, production, sales, and research more often than not leads to immediate reorganizations and long-term planning engagements.

"Government"

Government ownership casts a different light on both external and internal controls. When a government agency such as the FDIC takes over, a new set of game rules applies, predicated on government regulations and political priorities. Many are sound and were sorely lacking in the first place. Others merely add layers of administrative approval.

Consultants can be the bridge between the old and the new. They can assist new managers merge the company's needs with elaborate federal regulations. They can also educate and assist previous managers in coping with the myriad of new rules and priorities.

"Financial Institutions"

With financial institutions in a commanding position, the primary control objectives shift to preserving assets and short-term cash. Top executives unable to cope with such a shift often find employment elsewhere. In privately held companies, owners frequently adopt a "give-up" attitude and abdicate responsibility for operating results.

Once again, consultants are needed. On one side they act as intermediaries to assure the financial institution that assets and cash are being managed effectively. On the other, they take the adjustment burden off the business owner or remaining managers. Non-bank creditors also prefer to see independent consultants oversee company activities. This often leads to extended term management engagements that can last for months, even years.

Restrictive Federal and State Regulations

As both federal and state governments exert increasing pressure on businesses to conform to minority rights, safety practices, environmental protection, public health policies, employee rights, and tax laws, companies lose control over their own destinies. Massive amounts of money go into compliance expenses every year. Personnel who could contribute to the growth of the company dedicate their time to satisfying government auditors and inspectors. The control of marketing efforts, research, personnel, product design, exporting, and many other facets of a company's operation shift from company boardrooms to government bureaucrats.

Workable strategic plans must recognize these external controls. Long-range plans must be structured to take advantage of these regulations. Consultants offer a very real service by bringing to the table strategic planning methods that make use of government interference rather than avoiding it.

Dependence on Debt

The control of companies saddled with enormous LBO, anti-takeover, or misplaced expansion debt clearly rests with lenders rather than company management. Lenders dictate all manner of operating decisions: when and where to expand, expenditures for research projects, management compensation, dividend policy, acquisition and divestiture moves, and large capital asset additions.

Control has similarly shifted to investment banks and venture capitalists who have invested large sums of equity capital in a company. Representatives of these equity players often sit on boards, approve new management hires, insinuate themselves in management evaluations, direct equipment and facilities additions or disposals, and dictate dividend and compensation policies.

Independent consultants are in a unique position to offer services in a wide array of disciplines to satisfy both external and internal management. When friction arises, and it very often does between these external lenders/investors and company management, consultants can contribute sound operating and long-range recommendations recognizing the interests of both parties.

CHANGES IN RELATIONSHIPS AND VALUES

Ownership and control changes foster new relationships between management and employees, between the company and government bureaucracies, lenders, and major investors, between the company and the community, between financial institutions and government, between cultures, and between lawmakers and employees. A rapidly increasing awareness and acceptance by large and small companies of the need to be socially responsive casts a new light on the role the public plays in business decisions.

Although changes in relationships and values tend to create an immediate unsettling of company policies and, therefore confusion among executives and other employees, there is little argument that over the long haul business managers must learn to adapt. For example, in a recent survey it was learned that increases in salaries and bonuses have a lesser impact on managers and executives than congenial work environment, public recognition, and peer acceptance and support.

Wildlife advocates raised a public outcry against dolphins caught in tuna nets, and the tuna industry changed. Consumer councils publish lists of companies that are socially active and those that disdain social involvement. Many of the latter are feeling severe drops in sales. After the Valdez oil spill, for a while at least, consumers stayed away from Exxon gas stations, forcing price cuts from the parent.

Consultants have the opportunity to play a major role in transitioning companies to this new social paradigm, especially in the area of employee motivation. Several smaller companies are beginning to experiment with concepts of "community" in the work place, encouraging employees to rely on one another for everything from getting to and from the job, to performing work loads, to becoming involved in company policy decisions, to marriage counseling.

A few forward thinking consultants have begun to pick up the gauntlet, utilizing this concept for restructuring organizations and for developing employee incentive programs. Executives are especially susceptible to "community" dynamics as a motivational tool.

These radical changes in ownership, control, relationships, and values force senior managers to take a new look at company objectives, strategies, and procedures. Three- to five-year operating plans are no longer sufficient to encompass strategic diversification of markets and resources. Traditional organizational structures that load a company with bureaucratic fat prevent rapid changes in tactics as competition intensifies. Incentive programs from yesteryear no longer motivate managers beyond the short term.

Such redirection of corporate thinking without concurrent internal experience opens doors to management consultants well-versed in the new techniques and ideas that are necessary to bring these changes into focus. Traditional strategic planning, organizational development, and employee motivation engagements are rapidly giving way to a demand for assistance in recommending and implementing new management approaches to solving deficiencies in these crucial areas.

The three disciplines—strategic planning, organizational development and employee motivation—cannot be viewed as separate management activities. The success of corporate strategies depends on the capability of the organization to bring them to fruition. Organization effectiveness relies on motivated managers. Meaningful motivation tactics reflect corporate strategies. The interweaving of all three mandate an integrated approach to bringing a client into the twenty-first century.

Although strategic planning, organizational development, and employee motivation remain distinctly different disciplines, cutting-edge consultants must develop acumen in all three. One without the other two solves only one-third of the puzzle. General management consulting over the next decade must encompass all three disciplines even though a specific engagement may focus on one or the other.

From the consulting perspective, although slight variations exist, similar organization structures, fee schedules, marketing efforts, type and size of client, and production skills come into play for any of the three disciplines. Therefore, recognizing that specific engagements bear different titles, for the sake of simplicity, the remainder of this chapter addresses those aspects under the one heading of general management consulting.

CATEGORIZATION OF ENGAGEMENTS

Strategic planning engagements involve working with the client's board of directors, CEO, and other top managers to evolve a long-range plan for meeting the company's objectives in fulfilling its mission. The starting point involves clearly defining company mission. This sounds easy, but in reality is one of the most difficult parts of the engagement.

A client's mission may be to produce and sell high-quality widgets to the health care industry, to become a major force in the community, to pay continuously increasing dividends to its shareholders, to play a major role in public policy decisions, to be the predominant force in its industry, or any number of other possibilities. The sticking point is to get the client's top management to recognize and define, in writing, just what it is they are trying to do with the company.

Too often, varying agendas permeate the top management ranks. The board thinks the company's mission is one thing, the CEO another, operating executives a third, and so on. Without a clearly defined, mutually agreed upon mission it is impossible to develop company objectives, and hence a strategic plan.

Enter the independent management consultant. Capable consultants act as arbitrators, coordinators, stimulators, and "father confessors" to get the various management factions to agree on a company mission. This takes persuasive, and in many cases, negotiating skills. It takes patience. Above all, it takes a grasp of group dynamics and management psychology. Consultants must be smooth, non-abrasive, and non-argumentative. They must be knowledgeable about the methodology of company boards. They must cut through superfluous discussions and bring the single point of establishing a company's mission home to client management.

Once the client's mission has been established consultants can help the board and managers weigh alternative objectives for achieving it. Alternatives might include global expansion, the acquisition of operating companies, divestitures of existing subsidiaries or divisions, pruning or adding product lines or joint ventures, recapitalizing the balance sheet, restructuring product mix or customer mix, a new product development program, or anti-takeover measures. Not infrequently, project assignments emanate from strategic planning sessions. Inevitably, as objectives get firmed up the focus shifts to people.

Does the client have the right management team to make the objectives happen? Do managers have the background and technical skills? What training courses need to be implemented? Do communications flowing up and down the organization optimize decision-making? Are the various activities and functions organized properly to implement tactics necessary to achieve strategic objectives? Being an integral part of the strategic planning process and independent of company politics, the consultant should be in an excellent position to help resolve these issues by recommending efficient organization alternatives.

Organization Remodeling

Consultants specializing in traditional organizational development know all the theories advocating vertical, horizontal, cyclical, and central focus organizations. This is all valuable background experience but not enough. Consultants need a new approach to cope with changing multinational relationships within an organization. Decision-making, implementation, and communications within an organization must take into account varying cultural, language, image, and personal objective criteria.

The organization structure of the next decade will be bionic, modeled after the relationships of living organisms. Such a bionic organization incorporates instant electronic communications. It bends to internal and external pressure points without cracking. It emulates the self-healing properties of organic structures, one interrelated part taking up the slack from another temporarily damaged.

To recommend methods for building such an organization, consultants must be aware of how people communicate naturally, without artificial constraints but within the framework of company objectives. Planning the implementation of a bionic organization over a period of years involves a correlation of existing managerial talents with either retraining or recruiting from the outside.

Organization engagements frequently branch out into personnel evaluation projects. Staffing for global expansion intertwines with international consulting areas. Engagements calling for the integration of a client's organization with that of an acquired company or restructuring after a divestiture often evolve from M & A work.

Strategic objectives can only be met with the right organization. And to function at peak efficiency, managers within the organization must be properly motivated. This, in turn, leads to the third rapid growth niche in general management consulting: employee motivation programs.

Employee Motivation

Traditional incentive programs usually follow one of two paths: they either reward managers with cash bonuses and stock options for achieving predetermined sales, profit, or return on investment goals, or they are predicated on an annual subjective evaluation of personal achievements. Both have their place. However, they are not sufficient to motivate managers in a bionic organization. More subtle, indirect recognition that correlates both the personal objectives of managers and strategic objectives of the company, are needed. Innovative approaches that integrate a manager's needs and desires, not only for financial rewards, but also for public recognition, entrepreneurial freedom, company ownership, and family support ensure a person's best efforts on behalf of an employer.

Structuring the work environment to recognize a manager's interactive needs in a true "community" setting is one approach being developed and tested. Decision-making authority commensurate with responsibility for performance has long been recognized as an essential motivating tool. Only recently, however, is it being acknowledged within an organization framework. By steadily increasing their ownership share of the company, employees share the bad years with the good. This makes managers feel that they are important spokes in an integrated wheel. Concerned programs to correlate a manager's family needs and job requirements meet with almost instant company loyalty and increased motivational drive.

Consultants play a major role in recommending and implementing new forms of management incentives. Untouched by internal agendas, consultants can bring new ideas to the board and top management without fear of recriminations. Test programs can be implemented under the direction of consultants. Effectiveness evaluations can be performed. Individually designed incentive programs can be implemented to meet specific goals of each manager. As new managers come on line consultants can bring their suggestions for improvements to the attention of top executives without jeopardizing the managers' positions.

Over a period of time, effective motivation programs substantiate the effectiveness of new organization structures. Efficient organization structures hasten the implementation of tactics to meet the company's strategic objectives, and the loop is closed.

CONSULTING ORGANIZATION

General management engagements tend to be long-lasting; in fact, some never seem to end. Directions from and reporting to a board of directors that meets once a month or every two months can drag the engagement on for months, even years. Tracking down a CEO with a dozen or two balls in the air gets frustrating.

Implementing a radically new organization structure might take twelve months before all the bugs get worked out. If part of the engagement involves assessing a new employee motivation program it could take a year or more to definitively measure results. Add to these lengthy steps additional assignments that involve specific projects and it's easy to see how a consulting firm can remain symbiotically attached to a client for a very long time.

Fortunately, general management engagements are not usually continuous. Most do not require lengthy, contiguous stays at a client's office. When not performing specific tasks or participating in meetings you can easily pull back to your own office, as contrasted to project engagements requiring almost continual presence at the client's site. This recess leaves room for marketing or for production on other engagements.

The exception occurs when a client hasn't recognized, or accepted, the new strategic planning criteria, organizational concepts, or motivational approaches. Then a good part of the consulting job is trying to persuade the CEO, or the board, that traditional methods won't work any more. Chances are good, however, that if the client's leaders think along those lines, you won't get the engagement in the first place.

Both to create the "look right" image and to handle contingencies as they arise, consulting organizations should include at least two partners, and preferably three or four. Sole practitioners find that informal partnerships work better than consortiums or networking for this type of engagement. Clients want to feel comfortable that a consulting firm will remain committed to the job over the long haul. They don't want "partners" pulling off the assignment to handle other jobs, which frequently happens with either networking or consortiums.

Clients also want to be satisfied that the consulting firm is a legitimate business, not merely a few ex-executives taking up consulting in their spare time. Although consultants are famous for playing the mirror game, it won't work for this type of engagement.

In addition to demonstrating commitment by introducing several partners, consultants must also have a legitimate office and administrative personnel—a secretary and a computer operator as a minimum. It can be very embarrassing to have a potential corporate client call the office to discuss an upcoming general management engagement only to be confronted with an answering machine. A bionic office as described in Chapter 3 looks much better, especially if a client sports overseas ownership.

Other reasons support a multi-partner firm. If the client has several operating locations, either domestic or overseas, and you must travel to the remote sites, someone must mind the store at home. Very often one consultant works through problems at the client's home office while other partners handle remote locations. Extended term engagements also require partners to handle other clients and new marketing efforts.

A difficult general management assignment might require complete immersion. I took an engagement to help a client develop a global strategic plan and a top management reorganization. I became so immersed in the daily effort that I didn't see the light of day for six months, including weekends. If two partners in our informal partnership hadn't covered other clients for me, I could not have taken the engagement.

General management engagements usually call for consulting expertise in more than one discipline. Expertise required for developing global strategies is different from that needed to redesign an organization structure. Diverse operating divisions in manufacturing, distribution, and perhaps service or retail activities necessitate different consulting background. Consulting firms that can hold out expertise in such diverse areas as financing, engineering, production, and marketing are the ones that land the largest and highest paying clients.

Networking also comes in handy; but in addition to, not in lieu of partners. Because of my background in the financial area and extended experience in international markets I am frequently asked to handle a specific overseas project as part of a reorganization or strategic planning engagement for other members in our network. Occasionally such work can be combined with personal trips. Last year while visiting my daughter in the Peace Corps on a Pacific island, I did a country survey of two states in Micronesia and sourced local funding to help out a network member develop marketing strategies in the Pacific basin for a client.

TYPES AND SIZES OF CLIENTS

Certainly no hard and fast rule determines which types or sizes of businesses need general management services. Fortune 500 companies occasionally seek strategic or organizational consulting advice, although usually from "name" firms or academic personalities. Small companies, say with annual sales of less than $5 million, occasionally hire consultants to develop employee motivation programs or to assist in developing market or new product strategies. In most cases, however, these assignments follow traditional paths because the client isn't large enough, or rich enough, to implement long-range corporate strategies.

That leaves the entire mid-size market as potential clients. Pragmatically, however, additional factors further restrict the market. A company must maintain sufficient profitability and cash flow and a strong enough balance sheet to provide the flexibility necessary to support long-term growth strategies. It must be in an industry or market niche that offers possibilities for new products, market control, facilities expansion, or substantial cost savings. Financially troubled companies seldom enjoy the luxury of long-term planning.

A company must also offer an attractive work environment for qualified managers. If it can't attract quality personnel, too many constraints arise to merit meaningful long-range strategies.

Finally, the board members or top management of potential clients must first recognize the radical changes occurring in the business environment and, second, want to do something to take advantage of these changes. These top executives must be forward-thinking, placing long-term market share above short-term profits. And they must be open-minded to creative employee motivation techniques that will probably be foreign to their experience. We all know that these characteristics eliminate many of our existing clients. It also further limits the number of potential clients we can go after.

MARKETING

Marketing clients in the general management niche must be viewed from a long-term perspective. These companies are run by smart managers, demanding the very best in consulting advice and assistance. Many have probably had a distasteful experience with less than capable consultants in the past and are gun-shy about trying this route again. Since they demand the best, less than professional advertising or promotion techniques turn them off.

Stay away from cold calls. The small probability of getting to a board member or the CEO makes these calls all but worthless. Even worse, the strong possibility of meeting with lower echelon managers with their own agendas could cut off viable opportunities for the future.

The best approach is to follow the process described in Chapter 4 for developing credentials as an authority. Granted, this takes time. It isn't something that happens overnight. Whether the path involves written or verbal communications depends on a person's abilities. Both methods get you to the same destination.

A consulting associate combined the two techniques. Through a personal contact he inveigled a summer teaching position in the school of business at a local university. He taught two courses: "Ethics in Business" and "Long-Range Planning." Two years ago he wrote a book, *Planning to Plan: Tips on Long-Range Planning for the Mid-Size Business*, which he self-published. It didn't sell, but that was all right, it was a small book and inexpensive to print.

He ordered 300 copies, mailing them to all his existing clients as well as those from the prior five years. Then he took a quarter-page advertisement in a national business magazine. Within four months he had sold over 100 copies of his book. More important, he received three calls from companies asking for appointments to discuss strategic planning engagements. This consultant swears that resultant fee income is already four times the cost of the book and the advertisement. Writing a book is an excellent way to establish credentials. But without a method for publicizing the book to the right market niche, it won't help attract clients.

Another approach to becoming an authority uses verbal communications. Getting on the speaker's platform at conferences attended by CEOs or high ranking executives provides about as high an exposure as you can get. Assuming you are an effective speaker, this route nearly always results in at least one client, sometimes many more.

Referrals from bankers, lawyers, public accountants, academicians, and trade executives also provide an effective way to tap new clients. The biggest drawback to relying exclusively on referrals, however, is that quite often the party making the referral does not fully understand either what the potential client wants or your unique capabilities.

I encountered this problem with a referral from the managing partner of a large local CPA firm. For years we had worked together on small business accounts. I wanted to expand my business into general management work. The CPA referred me to a $150 million client. I ended up with the engagement, but it was for a tax planning project, not general management consulting.

One of the best ways to ensure that the third party making the referral has a good idea of the type of engagements you want is to keep your professional contacts up to speed. This means allocating a fixed percentage of time every month to luncheons, dinners, meetings, and other contacts with lawyers, public accountants, bankers, and so on.

It goes without saying that contacts must be with individuals high enough in the organization to know the needs of potential new clients and to command the respect of top management in these client companies. The branch manager of a regional bank might be a good friend, but referrals from the bank should come from senior vice presidents or the president.

Excellent referrals come from prior clients. Even if the engagement involved a project such as a business acquisition instead of a general management assignment, satisfied clients end up providing the best concrete evidence of your personal traits and capabilities.

FEE STRUCTURES

Consultants traditionally charge hourly rates rather than flat fees for general management engagements. There is no reason to vary this practice merely because the engagement involves implementing new techniques. Hourly rates for mid-size clients run 50 to 100 percent higher than for project engagements.

Clients always want to know in advance how much the total job will cost. Each of us has our pet methods for estimating hours for project engagements. General management engagements utilizing strategic planning and organization approaches significantly different from traditional methods don't fall into the same category.

Clients expect implementation assistance as well as advice. When the implementation stretches over several years it's impossible to estimate total cost in advance. In addition, since implementation steps normally require board or at least CEO approval, which is difficult to obtain at other than scheduled meetings, billable hours remain essentially out of your control.

One way around this dilemma is to break the engagement into small segments. Each segment then becomes a project and project estimating procedures can be used. The biggest risk in doing this is that the engagement may be terminated at the end of any segment. Board members change their minds; the CEO retires; wars, floods, fires, or strikes put long-range plans on hold; any number of contingencies can occur that lead to termination. Instead of a long-term general management engagement you end up with short-term projects.

Another method calls for breaking the engagement into monthly or quarterly intervals. Prior to the beginning of the month or quarter estimate your hours for that segment. You may or may not hit them exactly but at least it gives the client something to budget. The same danger exists in this method as with the previous one, however. With a temporary sales drop, cash shortage, vacation schedule, or many other occurrences it's easy for a client to terminate your work for the next month or quarter until conditions improve. This not only breaks the momentum built up by both consultant and client personnel, it provides the client an easy escape from the full engagement.

An increasing number of consultants insist on long-term contracts with monthly or quarterly retainers. In some cases, this approach can salvage an engagement. For clients with questionable pay practices or facing financial difficulty retainers are the only way to go. Clients that are financially sound, however, frown on advance payments. If you don't trust the client to pay, why should the client trust you to perform?

Long-term contracts might look good on paper, and if you have to borrow working capital funds, contracts look good to bankers. However, any competent lawyer can find loopholes in nearly any contract. Two additional reasons indicate staying away from long-term contracts.

Personal and business conditions change over time. Perhaps political or economic changes dictate shifting to a different type of organization or to different market niches. A long-term contract acts as a straitjacket preventing flexibility when needed.

A perfect example occurred in the early 1980s when a consulting friend took a corporate reorganization engagement estimated to take eighteen to twenty-four months. The client had experienced several down years and to protect himself the consultant insisted on a twenty-four-month contract.

Within six months the opportunity arose for the consultant to head a major divestiture program for a Fortune 500 company. He wasn't getting very far with his client's reorganization program because of repeated obstacles from the company's managers. He asked the client to terminate the engagement. The client refused, citing their contract.

In the midst of a foreign acquisition engagement I learned that one of my children became very ill. I quickly turned the job over to an associate and flew home. Two years later I did another major acquisition for the same client. An iron-clad contract would have made it difficult to leave the first assignment and, under the circumstances, I probably would not have been asked to participate in the second acquisition.

A second, and in some ways more serious, deterrent to long-term contracts is that some clients feel bound to a contract once it is executed. This perceived obligation to continue with a long-term engagement when a client's needs change causes friction between client and consultant. Inevitably this results in an adversarial relationship hurting both parties. Far better for both sides to be free to continue or sever connections at will.

Scope agreements should always be executed for any type of consulting work. As pointed out in Chapter 3 a clearly defined written scope makes both client and consultant aware of the defined limits of the engagement. Long-term contracts, however, frequently lead to problems for both parties. General management engagements must be based on mutual trust if consultants are to be effective. A long-term contract removes the element of trust and replaces it with a potentially expensive and disruptive legal obligation.

FULL-TIME MANAGEMENT ENGAGEMENTS

The smaller the client the greater the likelihood that a general management engagement will turn into a full-time assignment, regardless of how it began. Although it can happen with any engagement, full-time assignments occur most frequently when they begin as an organization development job.

Inevitably, by the time the reorganization is completed, one or more key managers have either resigned or been laid off. Since by this time you have a fairly good understanding of the client's business, the CEO or business owner could ask you to fill the position while conducting the recruiting process. Suddenly you are making operating decisions rather than merely giving advice.

Obvious advantages in such an arrangement exist, such as generating more income and greater billable hours. Just as obvious disadvantages exist, such as not having time to service other clients or market new clients. Less obvious questions also arise. How do you maintain independence when in an operating position, representing the company to bankers, investors, financial analysts, customers, and suppliers? What effect does the loss of independence have on relationships with other clients or for getting new clients? What conflict of interest questions arise when you have other clients in the same industry? Questions of confidentiality also come up.

The greatest hazard in accepting a full-time operating assignment relates to performance liability. A prime example occurred when I accepted a full-time as position vice president of finance with a client for which I had developed a long-range planning procedure.

The previous financial vice president had resigned and we were having difficulty replacing him. The client's business required that the vice president of finance be a CPA and certify compliance with state and federal investment banking laws. During the six months that I held the position I authenticated several compliance reports. Eventually we hired a replacement and I returned to my other clients.

Four months later I received an angry call from the investment banking client, claiming that as his consultant, I was named as a co-defendent in a suit brought by a disgruntled lending institution. This institution was a third party to an LBO arranged by the investment bank. It took another six months to clear myself, plus legal fees. Never again would I take a full-time assignment from any client, regardless of its profitability. It just isn't worth the risk.

7 International Consulting Markets

International trade in goods and services reached more than $6 trillion in 1990, a 24-fold growth since 1960. Market demand for virtually every type of product and service from grain to computer software, from legal services to aircraft engines is growing at a faster rate than any single nation can possibly control. The need for debt and equity capital to support this growth also surpasses the ability of any single nation or group of nations to regulate its flow. Cross-border market demand and cross-border financing have become a way of life.

The traditional economic concept expounded by Adam Smith 200 years ago that the most efficient producer with the lowest price would be the most profitable just doesn't work any more. Countries the world over use tariffs, direct and indirect subsidies, and favored tax laws to foster the growth of their own producers. Complex regulations, licensing, and work permits inhibit, but cannot stop foreign competition. Instead of helping national companies, these barriers to free trade play havoc with internal markets. National attempts to control trade, capital, and resources are no longer effective.

Members of the European Community (EC) are searching for a middle ground through the use of joint ventures, cross-border ownership, worldwide resource sourcing, and global financing, to cope with national interests and still permit semi-free markets. These elaborate arrangements lead to even more extensive and complex negotiations with government bureaucrats, foreign business and banking leaders, and national power groups.

The world economy is experiencing a transition period. The power of old, national institutions, companies, and state leaders is giving way to a new world economic order, replete with international bureaucrats, financial institutions, and business conglomerates. How long the transition will take is anyone's guess, but the sheer magnitude of changes indicates confusion and jockeying for position at least through the next decade.

Consultants have an excellent opportunity to participate in these changing times. Institutions and organizations of every size and shape need help in a multitude of areas. As outsiders with no competitive advantage to gain over the players in this drama, consultants are the logical choice to help pave the way.

Governments need assistance in privatizing national companies and industries and in structuring licensing, tax, public health and safety, and other new regulatory standards. Public and private companies need help in solving an even greater array of problems: matching cultural tastes with product ingredients and advertising, sourcing and structuring joint ventures, restructuring organizations, planning strategic objectives, recruiting personnel, identifying market niches and market demand in various countries and regions, negotiating complex contracts, gathering data for foreign expansion, sourcing financing, acquiring or starting foreign businesses, arranging local business licenses, and cutting through bureaucratic red tape, to mention a few.

Companies entering global trade have no other choice. Without in-house international experience, they must use consultants for their initial thrust. Once engaged in global trade, many large and small companies alike continue to use consultants to fill the gaps in specific projects. With the globalization of trade and finance, the demand for experienced consultants is mushrooming faster than any other market niche.

This chapter examines consulting opportunities in the overall international sphere. Chapter 8 takes a closer look at three of the fastest growing specialized niches: international finance, countertrade, and country evaluations.

QUALIFICATIONS AND EXPERIENCE

No specialty demands more unique experience than international consulting. Yet the type of qualifying experience varies all over the lot. Negotiating a contract in Britain or Australia requires a different background than for assisting a business start-up in Argentina. Structuring a joint venture in Abu Dhabi can't compare to arranging for raw material exports from South Africa. Both the work to be performed and the country or region to which it relates determine how much and the type of experience and qualifications you need. Nevertheless, certain universal guidelines seem to exist regardless of what you do and where you do it.

International consultants should possess or have experience in:

1. At least two languages from among English, French, German, and Spanish. A smattering of Japanese, Russian, or Arabic is also desirable

2. Living abroad; at least one year, and preferably three to four, in the region covered by the engagement

3. Working abroad; preferably in the region covered by the engagement

4. Exposure to foreign banking and exchange rules

5. Knowledge of U.S. trade practices/barriers/laws affecting American companies doing business abroad

6. Personal contacts in legal and public accounting firms abroad, preferably in region covered by engagement

7. Personal contacts at the senior vice president level or higher in one or more U.S. money center banks, transnational foreign banks, and federal aid programs

8. Personal and business flexibility to take extended trips lasting two to three months

9. Soft negotiating skills, not hard

10. Demonstratable ability for discretion and confidentiality, far more than in the United States

11. Political connections in Washington; not essential, but very helpful

The importance of personal contacts cannot be overemphasized. When handling engagements in the United States, your expertise, background, and capability should be enough to land clients and perform engagements. This is not the way it works overseas. Religion, prejudice, and political connections significantly influence the outcome of most international transactions. Government and business leaders, minor bureaucrats, and foreign laws continually change but the rules of the game remain constant.

It is difficult if not impossible to overcome these biases. Therefore, smart international consultants learn how to turn obstacles to their own as well as their client's advantage. This can be done most efficiently by knowing the right people in the right places. The right places are the points of power. In international trade, these power points reside in U.S. and foreign government trade offices, international trade groups (e.g., international development banks, United Nations trade departments, European Community agency offices, etc.), and international foreign banks (e.g., Dai-Ichi Kangyo, Sumitomo, Barclays, Credit Agricole, Swiss Bank Corp., Deutsche Bank, Hong Kong and Shanghai Bank) among others.

Foreign offices of American "Big Six" public accounting firms and multinational law firms provide an excellent entry to these power points. It takes some maneuvering and a little time and effort, but with perseverance, introductions can be arranged. Once the introduction is made it's up to you to discreetly develop a working relationship.

Consultants repeatedly ask me how to gain international experience. In one sense it's the chicken and the egg syndrome. You can't get engagements without experience; you can't get experience without engagements. Yet many sole practitioners as well as larger firms enter the international market every year. No magic formula defines the steps to qualify. Each individual and consulting firm must use the approach that works best for them. However, here are some ideas I have used myself and suggested to other consultants as possible paths to the international scene.

1. Read. read, read. A number of excellent books cover the rudiments of international trade. My book *Going Global: New Opportunities for Growing Companies to Compete in World Markets* is a good place to begin. Hundreds of international magazines can be purchased in any major book store. Many are published overseas and include information not otherwise readily available from other sources.

Publications from the World Bank, Eximbank, Department of Commerce, Department of State, and the Bank for International Settlements are excellent sources of current material. Most of the "Big Six" public accounting firms publish periodic newsletters on current international trade developments. Price Waterhouse and Arthur Andersen are especially helpful. Industry trade journals occasionally deal with international matters. The sources of reading material are unlimited.

2. *Attend international trade shows.* Nearly every month state or city trade bureaus or industry trade groups sponsor international trade shows. Many of these occur overseas. Many others are held domestically. Nearly all of the exhibitors and most of the attendees represent both domestic and foreign companies actively engaged in international trade. This provides an excellent opportunity not only to learn about activities in various industries and parts of the world, but also to do some marketing.

3. *Attend seminars/conferences on international trade.* Federal, state, and city trade bureaus and industry trade groups present a steady stream of seminars and conferences covering everything from shipping documentation to sourcing joint ventures, and from financing to market demand trends for products and services in specific countries. Many are technically oriented dealing with such topics as foreign sales corporations (FSCs), preparation of bid documents, project management, letters of credit, trade finance, and so on. Others stick with more general topics focused on marketing and advertising procedures for specific products or services. Still others use a more esoteric approach discussing roles and relationships of joint ventures, government aid, trade barriers, and the balance of trade.

4. *Take a course.* Several graduate schools of business now offer evening courses in various aspects of international trade. Many universities also offer periodic conferences on international trade subjects featuring renowned speakers and panelists. Some schools have excellent reference libraries with knowledgeable librarians to help locate information on specific international trade topics. Berlitz and several other language schools offer cram courses to learn a new language, at least at the conversational level.

5. *Travel.* Nothing beats the first-hand experience of being in a foreign country. If you don't have the opportunity to live or work overseas, sporadic traveling, on vacation or otherwise, gives you the flavor of a country or region and some knowledge of what it takes to survive there. While in a country pick up demographic, tourist, and trade literature at local government offices. Meet with the local office of the American Chamber of Commerce. Meet with executives of branches of American banks—Chase, Citicorp, Bank of America, etc.—or English banks.

If possible, set up appointments with local managers of divisions and subsidiaries of American or British companies, just to learn the ins and outs of doing business there. Meet with officials of export and other trade bureaus. These are all cold calls, of course, so don't expect to do much effective marketing. The main purpose is to get a flavor for that country's economic and trade circumstances and at the same time to make valuable contacts for future reference.

These techniques all work well as primer courses in international trade. It doesn't take long to become conversant with the peculiar requirements of the international arena and at least some of the idiosyncrasies of various countries. Nothing takes the place of actually living and working overseas, but all these steps have provided consultants a modicum of expertise, enough to confidently begin a marketing campaign.

COMPETITION

International consulting is fiercely competitive: but then any market yielding such a high income potential should be competitive. Competition comes from consulting firms located throughout the world. Competition also comes from academia. Eager to build a public name for themselves as well as pick up additional income, part-time consulting has been a favorite playground of college professors for years. Because of the political flavor of international consulting, many so-called experts are being engaged by foreign governments to assist in their transformations to market economies. Not to be outdone in the public eye, Fortune 500 companies also look to the college campus for consulting advice.

Ex-government bureaucrats have also entered the fray. Replete with political connections up and down the halls of the White House and the Pentagon, they remain in high demand as a medium to influence trade agreements and obtain lucrative contracts.

Engineering, architectural, and design firms the world over often get first crack at major international projects awarded by local governments and paid for largely by U.S. aid. Once through the technical door, they solicit additional non-technical work to structure joint ventures, recruit personnel, and a variety of other management projects.

Andersen Consulting, a division of Arthur Andersen & Co. is one of the world's largest management consulting firms with offices worldwide. With clients from audit and tax engagements, competing with this firm on their home turf is virtually impossible.

Not infrequently, international consultants work hand in hand with their own government bureaucrats. Consultants from the United Kingdom can count on government support ranging from introductions, to financing, to making the consulting engagement part of the financial or contract package. Government bureaucrats from France, Spain, and Italy are also notorious for insisting that their consulting firms be awarded contracts before granting financial aid or export credits to foreign buyers. Latin American countries are no different. Nor are Japan, Korea, or Taiwan. The only difference arises with consultants from the United States. To my knowledge, the U.S. government continues to disavow favoritism, at least publicly.

Where does this tough competition leave the sole practitioner or smaller consulting firm? In a very enviable position. While competitors fight over huge projects from large corporate and government budgets, except for Andersen Consulting and the consulting arms of other "Big Six" public accounting firms, few of these power brokers worry about smaller and mid-size clients. Since neither the fees nor the publicity matches major projects, the big competitors stay away. In addition, many large foreign projects require sub-contracts. Large consulting firms usually back off and let sub-contractors handle their own problems and, of course, hire their own consultants.

TYPES OF CLIENTS

International consultants service four broad types of clients:

1. Companies expanding into global trade, either through exporting and importing, or by establishing a foreign presence with manufacturing plants, distribution warehouses, service centers, or sales offices
2. Foreign companies expanding into the United States or using the U.S. as an intermediate transshipment point
3. U.S. government agencies involved in foreign aid
4. Foreign government bureaus responsible for developing infrastructure projects or for converting nationalized companies and industries to non-governmental ownership

Very often an engagement that begins in one category integrates activities from all four.

Excluding engineering and design firms that call themselves consultants and large, well-known firms such as McKinsey, Andersen, and Little, it's nearly impossible to get international work from large American or foreign companies. However, with the increasing recognition by smaller and mid-size companies that they must get into global trade to survive, plenty of business remains.

Engagements with foreign government agencies are also next to impossible for smaller, non-engineering firms to obtain. With some noted exceptions, favoritism for national consultants all but closes these doors. These exceptions generally arise with very small, independent states that are trying to develop their infrastructure and trade base to bring in hard currency. Some of the Pacific island nations and a few newly formed African states are good examples. As long as there isn't a colonial tie, governments in these nations look for consultants offering the best qualifications, synergistic religion and culture, and the lowest cost.

Other than these, developing nations are a tough nut to crack. They seem to fall into two categories.

1. Nations that remain in colonial status, those that are trust territories or protectorates, or those who depend on financial aid

from a mother country. They invariably give consulting jobs to firms from the mother country.

2. Nations that have recently gained their independence. They continue to select consultants from their previous parent.

Without political clout, other consulting firms find it nearly impossible to penetrate these prospective clients.

U.S. government aid agencies such as the Agency for International Development are equally difficult to penetrate without political influence. Occasionally, the Overseas Private Investment Corporation can be helpful in steering you in the right direction. At times the Inter-American Development Bank provides leads. Generally, however, working through the U.S. government requires more effort, time, and hassle than it's worth.

The best bet for sole practitioners or smaller firms is to concentrate on small and mid-size clients based either in the United States or in foreign lands.

MARKETING

Because discretion, confidentiality, and political influence play such major roles in international consulting, advertising of any sort often causes more harm than good. The best approach to getting clients is by referral from banks, government officials, lawyers, public accountants, or other consultants, just as in many other consulting niche markets.

As discussed previously, nothing beats traveling to the country or region that you are interested in to begin making contacts and gathering economic and trade information. Don't ask for leads at this point. Just introduce yourself and let it be known that you are in the international consulting field. Follow-up calls and letters confirm that you are available for consulting work and would appreciate their referral assistance.

A second and less desirable approach, though still an effective marketing tactic for soliciting overseas clients, is through direct contacts—in a sense, cold calls. The trick is to know where to go in a foreign country to get the names and phone numbers of prospective clients. Many sources of varying amounts of information exist in different regions of the world. Here are a few I have used to get leads.

1. *Commercial officers of U.S. embassies.* Varying levels of competence and cooperation make this an iffy sojourn but still worth trying. Some commercial officers are extremely competent and welcome the chance to brief a fellow American on local conditions. Others are either unaware of what is going on, or consider anything smacking of commercialism beneath them.

If you can locate a good one, commercial officers have access to local political, economic, and commercial conditions and generally know what companies might need your services. They can also give you the names and addresses of important local bureaucrats, professionals, and trade associations.

The relevance of such information depends on the country and the location of the embassy. The London embassy on Grosvenor Square is so large and bureaucratic that only cursory information filters through. I have never received any help other than a cordial cup of coffee. Conversely, the embassy office in Seoul was reportedly very helpful to two close associates.

2. *Local managers of American international banks.* Citibank, Chase, Bank of America, Security Pacific, First Interstate and a variety of other large American banks maintain branches throughout the world. Although recent hard times have forced the closure of several, if one happens to be in your country or region by all means make a call. Previous contacts made while on exploratory travels will certainly help. These branch managers all speak fluent English. Many are American or British.

I have never had a poor reception from any of them. On the contrary, I have garnered more specific leads from bank managers than from any other source. They know the local politics, which companies like to deal with Americans, which ones to stay away from, and names of the local bigwigs. On several occasions these leads have led to significant engagements with local divisions or subsidiaries of American based companies. They have also led to invaluable introductions to ranking government officials.

A letter of introduction from a banker back home is essential. A marketing package that includes evidence of your credentials and reference letters also helps. Such a package is crucial when you call on prospective clients.

3. American Chamber of Commerce offices. The American Chamber of Commerce (ACC) maintains local offices in over fifty countries and sixty cities around the world. As opposed to U.S. embassies, ACC offices exist solely as focal points for economic and business interests. Nationals staff many of these offices but all speak fluent English, and of course American business people are always welcome guests.

As a center of business interests, the ACC employs officials who know everything of importance going on in the business community. They have been excellent sources of leads, even setting up meetings, arranging for interpreters, and in one case providing transportation to an out of town meeting. If any organization can get you leads, the ACC can.

4. Ranking executives of American companies. Here again, receptions have always been cordial. The company you call on may not need your services but many times will recommend other national, or American, companies that could.

5. Trading companies. It can't hurt to become familiar with the major trading companies located in your country of choice. They may not be of immediate help in soliciting clients but are a good source of referrals later on. On the other hand, you might hit it lucky and get a few direct leads.

6. Agency for International Development. The U.S. Agency for International Development (USAID) staffs offices in developing countries worldwide. These offices work directly with local government bureaucrats to structure and monitor U.S. financial and technical aid to infrastructure and other local development projects.

The chief officer always speaks English. Because of their close ties to local government officials, these employees are the best source of leads for new government projects coming down the pike and for companies that are bidding on these projects. Many are American companies but more are third-country foreign or local.

7. World Bank offices. The World Bank maintains small offices in countries around the world. The competence and cooperation of the staffs vary considerably. Some are excellent; some terrible. These offices won't help very much with concrete leads, but they can fill you in on local political and economic conditions. Many also provide a modest amount of demographic and economic statistical data.

In addition to calling on World Bank offices, international consultants find it helpful to register their credentials with the World Bank headquarters at 1818 H Street NW, Washington, DC 20433. The Bank likes to approve any consulting firm or individual consultant hired by a borrower.

The Bank also maintains a data base of qualified consultants called, quite naturally, Data on Consulting Firms (DACON). Records of firms listed in DACON are available to representatives of Bank borrowers and member governments. On request, the Bank prepares lists of suggested consulting firms that it feels are qualified to handle the project under consideration. Typical services the Bank considers in the consulting domain include engineering, architecture, economics, finance, and management.

ORGANIZATION FOR A SOLE PRACTITIONER

Organizing a consulting business to handle international engagements is a difficult, costly, and at times frustrating exercise. A sole practitioner's organization must consist minimally of three elements:

- A permanent administrative employee.
- A bionic office as described in Chapter 3
- An effective consulting network

International engagements require long stretches away from the office. Someone must cover the telephone, handle administrative matters, smooth clients' feathers, and generally sustain the business while you are away. Part-time help won't do the trick. A high-caliber administrative assistant is crucial.

Many times, in fact most of the time in developing nations, you will not have access to secretarial or research help. All appointments, reservations, report writing, confirmations, cash management, and collections must be handled by your administrative assistant back home. This entails sophisticated methods for communicating back and forth in any corner of the world, both by voice and with data transmission.

An administrative assistant should be bilingual or have a flair for foreign languages. Calls from and to clients, appointments, and reservations involve communicating with people in other countries. They may speak English, but nine out of ten times it's very broken English.

Your administrative assistant must also be available at odd hours of the day and night. Vast time differences, split work days (as in the Middle East), and the observance of weekends on other than Saturday and Sunday make very long work weeks.

The administrative assistance should also be capable of transcribing reports to typed or key punched format accurately and timely. You can't afford to keep transmitting back and forth for corrections. It's also possible that on occasion your assistant will be called to a client's office. This necessitates a good appearance and professional demeanor.

Also, try to carry a duplicate office with you when traveling overseas. Poor telephone service, erratic electricity, and unreliable mail service in many countries prevents normal communications with your office. This is one reason international courier services have grown so rapidly.

To compensate, I find it handy to carry a laptop computer with word processing, financial analysis, and telecommunications software, a microrecorder, a complete set of office supplies, the official international airline guide, a typed listing of hotels in and around the area I'm in as well as in cities along the route, and, in some parts of the world, a digital pocket telephone.

An effective consulting network comes in handy in a number of ways. Two of the most important are:

- Skills required for the job
- Marketing and production at home

Very frequently, special skills that you just don't have are required for short periods. Perhaps computer programming, electrical engineering, tax knowledge, or audit procedures are necessary but not available locally. It's helpful to have a network of people with these skills who can be called upon for short projects.

Obviously, when overseas you can't do much marketing or production for other clients at home. A reliable consultant or consulting firm in a network (or a consortium) can at least manage the crucial elements until your return. One of the greatest hazards faced by sole practitioners in international consulting is the time away from the office. Without constant nurturing it doesn't take long for a client base to fade away. And major breaks in marketing efforts mean starting all over again from ground zero.

ORGANIZATION FOR A PARTNERSHIP

Ideally, international consulting firms should consist of at least two, and ideally three or four, partners. At least one partner should have had work experience overseas, and preferably have lived abroad as well. Either the same or another partner should be fluent in at least one foreign language. A second language is not crucial but it certainly helps both in attracting clients and when negotiating contracts.

Partnerships should maintain the same administrative and office capability described for sole practitioners. The office manager, or administrative assistant, will be in frequent communications with people in different countries and an ear for languages can be a big asset.

Ideally, in firms with three or more partners, two can travel together to solicit new clients, meet government bureaucrats and bankers, and negotiate contracts. As in other consulting markets, the "look right" is as important as the "be right." To prospective clients, and especially foreign clients, two people making sales calls look better than a solo. It adds an impression of depth of talent, assures clients of full commitment, and erases fears that the consulting firm doesn't have the personnel or the breadth of skills to do the job.

The impression of "bigness" goes over well with bureaucrats and gives your firm additional strength in gaining political clout. After losing a bid to the Saudi Arabian Monetary Agency for a New England client, I had dinner with two partners from a rival British firm representing a construction company from the Netherlands. They politely informed me that the reason they won the bid was that while one partner convinced SAMA officials that his personal contacts with the ECGD (Export Credit Guarantee Department) assured British financing, the other partner's connections with a ranking MP assured British government performance guarantees.

FEES AND NEGOTIATING ABROAD

With the exception of consulting firms from some of the Latin American countries and India, fee structures remain fairly uniform around the world. Little difference exists between fees charged by an Andersen Consulting office and a sole practitioner or small partnership, which is one reason international consulting is so lucrative for smaller firms.

The variety of engagements in international consulting is limitless. Some involve strictly project type work. Others stress general management. Still other consultants work as "middlemen" or brokers between government bureaus and companies. Management training, recruiting, organization work, business acquisitions and divestitures, structuring financing and joint venture partnerships, business start-ups, and a variety of other assignments are typical of international consulting engagements. Technical and engineering work is an entirely separate market.

Fees can either be based on hourly rates (generally two to three times the amount charged domestically) or flat project fees. Occasionally not-to-exceed limits must be negotiated. Retainers or advance payments are common and highly recommended by experienced international consultants.

However, collecting invoices billed to an American client requires the same collection efforts employed at home. Collecting from a foreign client, either a company or a government agency, is a different story. Getting paid by a foreign client can be a nightmare without the proper terms and conditions negotiated into the engagement contract. Four conditions must be clearly and unequivocally stated in the contract:

- How much the fees will be (either hourly rate or flat fee)
- When the fees will be paid
- How and where they will be paid

- The currency denomination

The first two need no explanation. The same fee structures and payment procedures used domestically apply overseas. How and where fees are paid and in what currency they are denominated are considerations unique to the international arena.

Exchange rate fluctuations can be either beneficial or devastating. On a long engagement, taking payment in local currency with a declining dollar can reap unexpected profits. The reverse occurs when the dollar rises against local currency.

Currency repatriation laws in the host country might prohibit removal of local currency from the country or might exact a sizable tax to do so. Other countries allow repatriation freely. Soft currency or hard currency also makes a difference. English pounds, German marks, French francs, and Japanese yen are easily convertible on world markets. Guatemalan quetzals, Soviet rubles, and Laotian kips are not.

Unless they plan to use the fee income within the country of origin, or intend to negotiate a countertrade arrangement, most international consultants insist on payment in U.S. dollars or other hard currency. Payment should be made with an irrevocable letter of credit (L/C), confirmed by a U.S. or other major international bank, and drawn on a bank in the vicinity of your home office. Any deviation from this arrangement can and frequently does cause major headaches.

Negotiating tactics in the international arena vary substantially from those used domestically, regardless of whether the contract is for consulting fees, engagement scope, client financing, government procurement, material purchases, labor recruiting, or any other transaction. In the United States we are accustomed to hard-nosed negotiations, lots of give and take on both sides, coming in high, settling for lower, threats of withdrawal, and so on. In some countries similar tactics work. In most of the world, however, a softer, more sophisticated approach is called for.

Entire books have been written exploring various alternatives and tactics for negotiating every conceivable type of contract. Most of us have already been involved in more contract negotiations than we can count and have mastered our own techniques to achieve what we want. It would be redundant to philosophize on the "best" or "worse" negotiating tactics here. A few guidelines seem to hold in international work, however, and are therefore worthy of mention.

1. Prepare for lengthy negotiations. If it should take two days at home, plan on two weeks overseas.
2. Learn the major cultural idiosyncrasies before beginning. If you don't have time to master culturally acceptable protocol, bring along a national to assist (local lawyers are excellent assistants).
3. Maintain your cool. Exhibit courtesy at all times regardless of how heated the debate becomes.
4. Be prepared for informal negotiation, over dinner, on the golf course, at the club.
5. Be patient. Let the negotiation run its course without pushing for resolution.
6. Write up the points agreed upon each day. Get both parties to sign off on your description before proceeding to the next point.
7. Share negotiating sites when the other party is not government affiliated. Let the opponent choose the first site. You or your client choose the next one.
8. Arrange for immediate communications with your client's office, legal or audit professionals, and technical specialists. Use a fax, telephone, or telex where available. Otherwise arrange for DHL or other international courier to stand by.
9. Assist in drafting final contract document.
10. Do not leave without a copy of the document.
11. Confirm all side agreements by telex or fax as soon as you return to your office or to that of your client.

JOINT VENTURES AND ASSOCIATIONS

In certain parts of the world and for specific projects, consultants find joint ventures or informal associations with national consulting firms to be helpful, and in some cases essential, in getting clients and performing the engagement. The following circumstances frequently dictate a working relationship with a national consultant:

1. Large clients who already have a relationship with a national consulting firm
2. Technical expertise or specific experience not resident in your firm
3. Local conditions, political affiliations, and customs require local participation
4. Too large a project for one firm to handle but beneficial when two or more parties join together
5. National participation required by local laws

Marketing

If you get involved in several, widely separated countries or regions marketing can be a nightmare without local help. It's impossible to solicit clients in Europe, Latin America, and Southeast Asia simultaneously. The distances are just too great. Even if the final engagement doesn't require an association with local consultants, the pure marketing aspect does. Local consultants know the region. They know the character of local companies. They know which ones should be receptive to consulting solicitations. They also know which government projects are coming down the pike.

Legal Requirements

Local associates can be invaluable for getting appropriate licenses and registrations. They can help prepare bid proposals and translations. Local consultants follow the shifting of local politics and can be instrumental in clearing legal and trade barriers. They know which professional firms to use when needed. Local consultants might be helpful in coping with language and dialect barriers. And finally, they can be essential in assisting in the presentation and negotiation of contracts.

Contractual Agreement

The major difference between joint ventures or associations with consultants overseas and domestic consortiums, informal partnerships, and networks is that the foreign arrangement is for a specific project, client, or time period. In addition, it should be based on a contractual agreement, legally binding on both parties.

The contract should include agreements on the following topics:

1. Definition of activities to be performed by each party including the preparation and submission of reports to clients
2. A beginning and an ending date
3. Liability of each party
4. Methods for pricing services rendered, and billing and collection procedures
5. Sharing of profits and losses
6. Responsibility for payment of local taxes
7. Responsibility for record keeping and compliance reporting
8. A clear definition of standards to be followed in soliciting clients and performing engagements

It's crucial to draft and execute the agreement with the blessing of your attorney from home as well as a local attorney familiar with national laws and customs. Translations of the contract should be in English as well as in the local language.

Locating a Foreign Partner

Locating a partner or associate in industrialized countries is a snap. They are formally listed as consulting firms with names and addresses in local telephone directories. A straightforward request by letter or phone call gets the ball rolling. These consultants also attend local trade shows and conferences. Any competent lawyer or banker can make referrals.

The same holds true in several developing nations. Many qualified consultants reside in Caribbean, Central American, and several South American countries. They may be associated with universities or government bureaus. Again, local bankers, lawyers, and public accounting firms can be helpful for getting referrals. These are also good sources in many Pacific Basin developing countries, India, and Pakistan.

Locating qualified partners in African and some Middle Eastern nations is another story. Some very severe problems exist in several of the sub-Saharan Africa countries because of massive corruption in government circles and the lack of a broad educated class. Consultants in those nations with close ties to previous European colonial parents can usually be sourced through European referrals, but in other countries no easy way exists.

Some consultants find that appointing a legal representative is a smoother path than trying to locate a partner. Local representatives can be individuals or companies. In developing nations, government bureaucrats often take on representation status. A national accounting firm or law firm can be a representative, as can an executive from a manufacturing or distribution company. It is not unusual for local ordinances to require consulting representation long after the engagement ends.

A representative takes care of paying taxes, complying with government regulations, translations, authenticating bank accounts, and registering the consulting firm's business name. Representatives normally are not a good source of assistance for soliciting clients or for performing an engagement, although at times they can be. A formal, legally binding representation contract must be executed to prevent the representative from exceeding his authority and for protecting you in the event of law suits or government claims. All of which brings up a crucial subject for international consultants: professional liability.

Liability Protection

Although lawsuits against consultants for professional negligence are as uncommon overseas as they are in the United States, the frequency seems to be escalating. The major difference rests in potential damage to a consultant's reputation which would diminish chances for future work in the country. Some governments have also been known to refuse business permits to consultants who have had lawsuits brought against them, whether the suit was justified or not and whether the consultant won the case or lost.

No sure-fire way exists to prevent frivolous suits. Disputes with clients over collections, engagement scope, and interfaces with government officials seem to be increasing dramatically in some of the very poor, developing countries. Although constantly communicating with the client and carefully performing the job against a written scope contract mitigate potential suits, they cannot be entirely eliminated.

The best answer is to carry professional liability insurance coverage from the United States, with riders attached covering foreign suits. Two of the consistently best insurers have been CIGNA Insurance Co. of New York and Lloyd's of London with offices worldwide. These insurers can also secure a performance bond for you if necessary, or standby letters of credit from banks in place of bonds.

HOT GLOBAL MARKETS AND INDUSTRIES

Organization structure, skills, personal life style, religious and ethnic background, and mobility heavily influence where to search for international engagements. Travel time and accessibility, local prejudices, project and management skills, family concerns, personal health, and size of organization dictate whether to go after general management clients in sub-Sahara Africa, systems projects in Malaysia, or finance sourcing in Europe. A comfortable level of risk, language barriers, and political contacts also weigh heavily on the decision. The political and economic climate in a country or region obviously plays a major role.

The dynamic nature of the global economy makes a definitive listing of the best industries to target over the next decade impractical. The same holds true for a definition of the most likely countries for concentrated marketing efforts. However, for the foreseeable future certain industries obviously lead the pack and specific regions appear to offer higher potential than others.

Five of the hottest non-engineering international consulting markets that offer significant opportunities for the future are those American and foreign companies engaged in:

1. Infrastructure construction of all types—electricity generating and transmission; water drilling, pumping, distribution and purification; the building of roads, schools, hospitals, government offices, airports, and rail lines
2. Military hardware and software
3. Toxic and non-toxic waste disposal

4. Travel facilities—hotels, restaurants, rental cars, mobile offices, health clubs

5. Communications equipment and systems—satellite, telephone, underwater cable, television

Although your personal preferences, skills, and organization ultimately determine what regions of the globe offer the most potential, the following countries and regions offer unusual opportunities now and for several years to come:

1. Eastern Europe. Companies of all sizes and industries are zeroing in on development, service, and retail markets of eastern European countries, except for Rumania. In the not-too-distant future Rumania will also probably join the club.

2. The Caribbean, Central America, and Mexico. U.S. government self-interest will continue to strengthen these regions with economic aid. Close proximity, language familiarity, and lack of trade barriers are opening doors to many small and mid-size companies.

3. South America. Except in Peru, Colombia, and a few smaller countries, economic development is progressing rapidly. Trade agreements with the U.S. and the beginning of political stability encourage mid-size and larger companies to risk the challenge. Special financing arrangements also offer incentive.

4. Indonesia and Malaysia. Indonesia still has a long way to go to develop economic self-sufficiency. Malaysia is much closer. Both countries offer industrial and tourist development opportunities for the next decade.

5. Pacific island nations. Overlooked by large companies because of great distances and small population centers, many of these small countries desperately need products and services of all types. Aid from the United States, Europe, and Japan provides enormous financial reservoirs to be tapped by smaller and mid-size companies.

The "super" international development banks—Inter-American Development Bank, Asian Development Bank, and the European Bank for the Development and Reconstruction of Eastern Europe—provide excellent sources of upcoming projects and referrals to prospective clients. Consultants should register their skills, credentials, and capabilities with each. The European Development Fund (Brussels) is a good source for clients in African, Caribbean, and Pacific nations participating in the Lome Convention.

The World Bank maintains a data base of consulting firms wishing to do work in specific areas and, as previously mentioned, registering here might help. Personal contacts in the U.S. Agency for International Development and Eximbank nearly always yield client referrals.

The previously described intense competition among global consulting firms for government contracts and large corporate clients precludes most smaller firms from targeting these projects and companies. However, a mushrooming number of smaller and mid-size American and foreign companies are targeting these markets in developing regions. These are the prospective clients to concentrate on; leave government jobs and Fortune 500 jobs to the big firms.

International Financing, Countertrade, and Administration Market

8

One of the biggest stumbling blocks faced by companies entering global trade is how and where to arrange appropriate financing. Whether exporting from the United States or another country, starting up a division or purchasing a going business in a foreign land, or sourcing materials and labor off-shore, new capital must be raised. This may take the form of short-term working capital, long-term debt, or equity investments. The sources of international funds span the globe. The forms of capital and bank instruments are different from those found in domestic financing. The web of international finance creates a new spectrum of terminology, capital structures, and collateral requirements that most companies new to the international scene find extremely confusing.

Many American and foreign companies alike find that these hurdles seriously delay their entrance to global trade or deter them from even trying. Management consultants with a choice of financing alternatives at their fingertips find a lucrative market whose growth shows no sign of abating.

Although plenty of competition exists from public accountants, merchant bankers, and government bureaucrats eager to counsel larger companies, very few maintain a data base of options for smaller firms. Even the Export-Import Bank of the United States (Eximbank) concentrates on large exporters. International investment banks won't talk to a smaller company about initial global financing. If approached directly, the central export banks of Europe and the Far East frequently shuffle requests from smaller companies to the bottom of the pile. Foreign development banks tend to do the same.

Nearly all facets of international trade are conducted surreptitiously. In most cases, successes in customer solicitations, contract negotiations, money transfers, obtaining permits and licenses, and arranging financing are a result of intermediary connections rather than straightforward actions.

Larger companies maintain a network of worldwide representatives to ensure the retention of bureaucratic and professional connections. Smaller companies don't have this luxury. As neophytes in global business, most smaller companies don't have managers sufficiently experienced in international finance to even know where to begin. This makes consulting services invaluable and in many cases a necessity for doing business abroad.

With the globalization of money, companies involved in international trade must raise their capital from the least expensive, most readily available sources regardless of the location of the lender or investor. Money knows no national boundaries. Cross-border financing is already a reality in virtually every industry and for practically every type of international trade transaction.

One of the unique features of global trade is that marketing and financing go hand in hand. It's not enough to offer a customer the highest quality product, best delivery, and lowest price. Sellers must also offer to finance the transaction. A high percentage of international sales are culminated not because of product brand or price, but because a seller offers the most lucrative financing package.

Consultants can present clients a wide array of U.S. and foreign financing sources to choose from. They can help clients evaluate the right combination of financing options to meet strategic goals. And consultants can negotiate with lenders and investors to secure the best terms and conditions.

Selling to customers in developing nations presents a special financing problem. Whether importing from the United States or producing goods and services locally, soft currency nations generally cannot pay in U.S. dollars or other hard currency. This frequently means that if a company wishes to do business in one of these nations it must either arrange financing from outside the country or submit to one of many countertrade arrangements.

Most smaller and mid-size companies, however, are ill-equipped to negotiate a countertrade deal or to administer it once culminated. Consultants can assist in recruiting and training an international staff to administer countertrade agreements. They can also negotiate countertrade contracts, arrange with third parties for disposal of traded goods, and guide clients through the maze of host country, third country, and United States regulations affecting the transaction.

A second major stumbling block for smaller companies is selecting countries or regions that offer the greatest opportunities, and then coping with their respective legal, political, and trade anomalies. For example, assume a manufacturer of plastic dinnerware and eating utensils wants to begin an export program now, followed by a start-up of a foreign manufacturing plant in two years. The CEO believes the Caribbean offers the best opportunity but doesn't know the area well enough to pick a country.

A consultant works through a global strategic plan with the client leading to Barbados and the Grenadines as the most likely choices. After exporting for two years the client decides to open a manufacturing plant in Barbados. The consultant gathers sufficient data to determine legal requirements, trade barriers and incentives, labor availability, export restrictions, audit and tax regulations, and a variety of other critical matters before the client makes the move. This gathering of data, some from sources in the United States, some directly from Barbados, is called a country survey.

Financing engagements, countertrade projects, and country evaluations and surveys are complex undertakings. Successful completion requires astute negotiating ability. It requires connections in financial circles around the world. It requires the ability to sort through a myriad of political, finance, and trade barriers. These projects are not overnight or one-week exercises. Many take six to nine months to bring to fruition.

On the flip side, very little competition exists in this unique specialty. Large consulting firms, well positioned to handle finance and administration assignments, have concentrated their efforts where the fees and the likelihood of repeat business are greatest: with large, multinational corporations already engaged in international trade or with U.S. government-sponsored venture funds (such as those in Poland and Hungary). Enormous numbers of smaller and mid-size companies trying to compete in the global arena without international finance experience have been shunted off to smaller consulting firms.

FINANCING ENGAGEMENTS

Helping clients arrange financing for exporting out of the U.S., importing into the U.S., acquiring or starting a facility overseas, and exporting and importing between foreign countries is a good place to begin developing an international client base. Few smaller companies have any idea where to look for financial help. Nor are they cognizant of the many options available both within the United States and abroad. Most never think of using foreign public issues to raise capital or sourcing funds from private investors. In fact, many companies, both American and foreign, remain unsophisticated in international trade credit techniques.

Nine activities comprise the bulk of international financing engagements:

1. Selecting the right domestic bank to handle international transactions

2. Structuring trade credit with letters of credit, banker's acceptances, and other instruments

3. Arranging and negotiating loans from American and foreign banks

4. Coordinating loans, guarantees, and insurance from U.S. government agencies such as Eximbank, the Overseas Private Investment Corporation (OPIC), and others

5. Preparing and submitting applications for loans and guarantees from foreign export-import agencies

6. Raising capital from private sources

7. Coordinating equity and debt issues on foreign exchanges with investment and merchant banks

8. Negotiating debt/equity swaps

9. Designing and implementing accounting and other internal controls and cash management procedures for overseas projects

Bank Participation

Every facet of international trade requires the use of banks. They perform an array of services geared specifically to transacting cross-border trade, most of which are unheard of for domestic business. Credit extensions to buyers, payment guarantees, currency exchange, seller transaction working capital financing, performance guarantees, wire transfers, currency arbitrage, reference letters, coordination with government financial aid agencies, shipping documentation, and a myriad of other activities must flow through banking channels. The financial staffs in most smaller companies do not have the breadth of experience to handle these matters internally and look to consultants for guidance through the labyrinth.

The first step in helping a client cope with international finance is to line up a bank that has the appropriate expertise. Many smaller banks have not yet staffed to handle international transactions. Many more do not have an appropriate network of correspondent banks around the world. And many are afraid to support a customer in international finance without constant advice from another, more savvy bank. To avoid confusion, excess cost, and unnecessary time lags, it's necessary to search out banks with the following characteristics:

1. The bank must have an experienced, diversified international department. Without this expertise, it will be nothing more than an intermediary for another larger bank.

2. Decision-making bank executives must be familiar with the international roles of letters of credit (L/Cs), banker's acceptances, forfaiting, and other forms of buyer and seller credit.

3. The bank must accept Eximbank and SBA guarantees as collateral to loans. Banks must carry 10 to 20 percent of the loan balance under any government agency guarantee. The right bank will agree to do this without requiring additional collateral or personal guarantees.

4. The bank must be large enough to be recognized in foreign banking circles. It should maintain a network of correspondent banks in foreign countries, especially in the country the client will be trading in. Using a money center bank as an intermediary costs more and confuses transactions.

5. The bank must be organized to handle foreign currency translations, currency arbitrage (if necessary), and wire transfers directly to and from other banks around the world without going through a money center bank. The greater the variety of international services it offers the better.

Letters of credit (L/Cs) are the backbone of international trade finance. Everyone uses them in every country. Their two primary uses are as a payment device enabling a shipper to receive cash upon presentation of proof of shipment, and as a guarantee against performance, either physical performance as with a surety bond (called a "standby" L/C), or payment performance by the buyer.

Letters of credit used as payment devices come in many forms— revocable or irrevocable, confirmed or advised, payable at sight or over an extended period of time. L/Cs may be straight or negotiated, transferable, assignable, or restricted. They can be written to include or exclude virtually any specific provisions. L/Cs cover partial shipments, full shipments, or transshipments, applicable to one shipment only or revolving, covering many shipments. They may read "clean on board," "about," or "approximately" (referring to quantities shipped).

L/Cs must be properly prepared and executed to be valid. All supporting documentation specified in the L/C must accompany it for payment. Shippers use back-to-back L/Cs, off-balance sheet credit extension, assigned proceeds, or transferred L/Cs to raise export working capital.

If a foreign buyer can't raise the capital or credit to place a confirmed, irrevocable L/C as immediate payment, other bank instruments are available. Clean or documentary banker's acceptances (BA) are two such instruments. Forfaiting, the global equivalent of factoring receivables, is also a handy device.

Companies that find these techniques lacking might consider lease financing, especially if the sale involves capital equipment. A number of possibilities exist in structuring cross-border leases, many yielding a higher profit than standard financing procedures. Very frequently, a countertrade arrangement accompanies a lease program to convert the buyer's soft currency lease payments into hard currency.

International development banks are another excellent source of financing overseas ventures. The four coordinating banks work with local development banks and commercial banks to provide loans and guarantees to companies starting up a new facility, acquiring an existing business, or forming a joint venture with a local partner.

The consultant's role in arranging and negotiating bank loans, guarantees, and seller or buyer trade credit is advisory. The client must actually perform the implementation of L/Cs and other instruments and must accumulate shipping documentation. Consultants should lead the way, however, and assist in structuring appropriate instruments and making necessary contacts in appropriate quarters.

U.S. Government Financial Aid Programs

The U.S. government funds several programs that provide financing and technical assistance to exporters. A lesser number apply to direct foreign investment. On the export side, the Export-Import Bank of the United States (Eximbank) is the primary vehicle for financial aid.

Eximbank is an independent, corporate agency of the federal government. It provides financial and technical aid for the sale of most export products except shipments to Communist countries and military products or services.

Exporters must answer five questions in the affirmative to participate in Eximbank programs:

1. Is a U.S. export involved?
2. What foreign competition exists, and is it officially subsidized?
3. Is the transaction economically feasible?
4. Is there reasonable assurance of repayment?
5. Would voiding the transaction create an adverse effect on the U.S. economy?

Small businesses, however, are not required to prove foreign competition, providing the Eximbank's share of guarantees and loans totals less than $2.5 million.

Eximbank has established a "hotline" counseling service to answer questions from consultants and their clients about financing and other export assistance. The toll free number is (800) 424-5201.

Within Eximbank's commercial bank guarantee program, a company can get guarantees of up to 90 percent against short-term working capital bank loans and 100 percent against medium and long-term bank loans to foreign buyers (after a 15 percent down payment). Eximbank also makes direct loans to foreign buyers and "standby" loans to intermediaries (financial institutions). The Engineering Multiplier Program loans and guarantees apply to engineering design and construction projects and can range as high as $10 million.

Eximbank also offers credit insurance against buyer non-payment and foreign expropriation through the Federal Credit Insurance Association (FCIA).

Other federal agencies also provide export financing assistance. The Department of Agriculture offers aid to exporters of agricultural products through its Commodity Credit Corporation. The Small Business Administration (SBA) offers assistance through its Export Revolving Line of Credit (ERLC) program which can be combined with Eximbank guarantees.

One federal source of financing assistance for direct foreign investment is the Overseas Private Investment Corporation (OPIC). OPIC promotes private sector economic growth in over one hundred developing countries by offering assistance to U.S. companies wishing to start-up or acquire businesses in these nations. This assistance is targeted to smaller businesses, not large corporations. In addition to financial aid, OPIC maintains an investor information service and a network of investor missions around the world to help identify private investment and market opportunities.

Financially, OPIC provides medium to long-term project loans and political risk insurance. Any American company beginning or expanding an overseas project can qualify, providing the project meets OPIC's criteria. OPIC also finances the start-up of overseas leasing companies and offers contractor performance guarantees as collateral to bank standby L/Cs in place of surety bonds.

Private Financing Sources

One of the most popular private sources for financing export trade is the Private Export Funding Corporation (PEFCO). PEFCO was formed by several U.S banks and large corporations to supplement federal long-term financing for foreign buyers of American exports. Closely associated with Eximbank, PEFCO extends credit for export orders requiring longer term financing than a commercial bank will handle, but shorter than provided by Eximbank.

Joint ventures, either with foreign nationals or U.S. companies, present unique financing arrangements for starting or acquiring foreign businesses as well as cross-border trade. Many joint ventures are currently being formed with the larger company furnishing the money and the smaller partner taking on the performance and market risk. As noted in the previous chapter, consultants can play a major role in locating joint venture partners and in structuring the deal to incorporate financing as well as marketing advantages.

The whirlwind development of new, free-market economies has stimulated the formation of U.S. government-supported private venture capital funds. One of the first to begin operations was a venture fund started by forty American corporations, and backed with guarantees from OPIC, to provide funding for the privatization of Polish industries and the development of Polish infrastructures. Hungary benefits from a similar fund.

As free-market economies begin evolving in the Balkans, the ex-Soviet republics, China, and certain African and Latin American nations, it seems inevitable that additional U.S. government-supported programs and venture funds will be announced. Consultants offer the best line of communications for clients to get in on the ground floor. They can also keep tabs on what projects are coming up for bid and for other direct investment opportunities in specific countries.

Multinational Organizations

In addition to federal programs, several multinational organizations offer financing and technical assistance. Organizations such as the World Bank and the International Monetary Fund, funded by a conglomeration of nations, provide financial assistance directly to governments of developing nations, which in turn filters down to the private sector. Several agencies within the World Bank also offer financial assistance directly to the private sector.

The International Finance Corporation (IFC) coordinates and assists in arranging financing for joint ventures in developing nations. It also provides equity investment and/or partial debt financing to expand companies already established in these countries.

The International Development Association (IDA) offers financing very similar to that of the IFC, except that loans extend for a maximum of fifty years instead of the IFC's ten year limitation.

The International Bank for Reconstruction and Development (IBRD), a hybrid international development bank, lends directly to governments for infrastructure projects and other major development programs. It offers long-term, low-interest loans to finance the construction of roads, power plants, steel mills, and other capital-intensive projects in a developing country. Although the funds flow directly to governments, not the private sector, IBRD helps smaller companies identify projects that qualify for its financial aid.

It is virtually impossible for smaller companies to approach these organizations directly. Consulting intermediaries offer the best means. A consulting firm with connections in either the World Bank or the International Monetary Fund can corner this very lucrative, but small, market niche.

Foreign Government Financing Assistance

Once a company has an established facility overseas, a number of foreign government programs are available for short and long-term financing of both trade and expansion. Funds flow from the country's government-owned central bank, through agencies similar to Eximbank, and are available for exporting products to the U.S. or to other nations, for importing products into the country, for making cross-border direct investments, and for foreign credit risk insurance.

Most European programs emphasize credit insurance, supplemented by direct financing assistance. In the East Asia the reverse occurs. England, France, Germany, Japan, South Korea, and Taiwan all have financing programs that in many respects are superior to Eximbank.

Once again, smaller companies have little luck approaching these government-controlled organizations directly. Consultants act as intermediaries to make the application, negotiate the deal, and assist clients in monitoring compliance with the programs.

Public Markets

Public financial markets offer another avenue for financing overseas expansion providing a company is large enough to employ qualified financial managers. Capital raised through debt or equity issues on foreign exchanges can be either in eurodollars on European exchanges, yendollars on the Tokyo exchange, or local currency on other world exchanges. Either larger American investment banks or foreign merchant banks handle the details, but consultants help select the right bank and negotiate the terms of the issue.

Other possibilities also exist. Currency and interest swaps, zero coupon bonds, debt/equity swaps, and a variety of other methods are available for raising large sums of capital in world markets. Consultants involved in a company's strategic planning process can provide invaluable services by evaluating each alternative in light of the client's objectives.

COUNTERTRADE ENGAGEMENTS

If consulting assistance is helpful to clients trying to raise international capital, it is absolutely essential in the esoteric world of countertrade. Most smaller companies have never heard of countertrade, or if they have it has been in reference to multi-billion dollar sales of aircraft, military hardware, or primary infrastructure projects.

Even in those rare cases where client personnel can define the various types of countertrade, unless the company is currently using the technique, chances are high that they would not be able to source, negotiate, and administer a countertrade transaction. Consultants provide the only medium for companies to enter into and successfully conclude a countertrade contract.

Countertrade is a very simple concept and has been used since caveman days. In its simplest form, countertrade is barter. I repair your car. In exchange, you prepare my tax return. In its complex state, a countertrade transaction involves multiple parties, companies, individuals, and government agencies, all exchanging something they have—cash, services, or other products—for something they get in return—cash, services, or products. Countertrade transactions may extend over a few months, or they could go on for many years.

Why would companies get involved in such complex machinations? Because in some parts of the world it is the only way to compete. Trading in China, Eastern Europe, the ex-Soviet republics, many Latin American countries, and nearly all of Africa, or any country where hard currency is at a premium, requires a willingness to receive payment in forms other than cash, letters of credit, promissory notes, drafts, or bills of exchange.

Countertrade transactions are generally structured into one or a combination of six arrangements: barter, compensation, counterpurchase, offset, buy-back, or co-production.

The oldest form of trade, barter, means trading a quantity of one commodity for a quantity of another: eight horses for three cows, four gas turbines for 1,000 acres of land, 5,000 bushels of wheat for 40 cases of vodka. Obviously, once your client gets the exchanged merchandise it must either be used or sold.

Compensation is a modern form of barter involving a third party to dispose of the traded merchandise. Compensation transactions fall under a single contract, often making the transaction cumbersome to administer.

Counterpurchase is a variation on the barter theme that involves actual cash transfers. The foreign buyer arranges independent financing and pays cash for the products. The seller concurrently agrees to purchase goods that the buyer produces, over a period of time, for cash. The seller must then turn around and sell these goods to recover the purchase price and profit.

Offsets are used primarily by larger companies for the sale of capital goods. The customer is frequently a sovereign government using offsets to improve its foreign exchange position. An offset deal normally involves a package of transactions, carried out over a defined period of time. Theoretically, at least, it compensates the acquiring or importing country for loss of jobs, currency, and local development of technologies.

Buy-backs are typically used in the turnkey construction of infrastructure projects or manufacturing plants. Buy-back means that the contractor agrees to buy-back a certain percentage of the production from the new facility that has been built. The contractor then sells the products and reaps any profits.

Co-production transactions require the contractor to take an equity interest in the turnkey project or furnish management support as partial compensation. A host country contractor and a foreign contractor share the construction, with both parties sharing in the facility's ownership. Operating the facility is known as co-production since both parties remain responsible for the production of products and both parties benefit from their sale.

It's easy to see that countertrade, regardless of its form, is not something companies enter into haphazardly. It is complex, risky, and long-term. But it's an important and growing niche for consultants.

Consultants perform five services in a typical countertrade transaction. They assist the client to:

- Structure and negotiate a countertrade transaction
- Recruit and train internal staff to source countertrade customers and then to administer the contract
- Locate appropriate third parties to dispose of the traded goods
- Monitor the performance of countertrade partners
- Develop a strategy to utilize the countertrade exchange for expansion into other product lines or businesses

Consulting Qualifications

No special training is needed to get into this specialty. Once established as an international consultant, it's almost impossible not to become involved in a countertrade transaction fairly early in the game. A few preliminary steps should be taken, however, to be ready for a countertrade engagement when it comes.

Clearly, the first step is to understand the different variations of countertrade transactions. Although countertrade transactions are relatively new to smaller companies, the major transnationals, especially the aerospace and military hardware companies, have been involved in countertrade for years. A fast way to get up to speed is to ask for a meeting with the countertrade specialist in one of these large companies. If approached properly, most are anxious to relate their knowledge.

Another good approach is to read everything you can get on the subject. Not too many books have been written on the subject, but there are a few. *Winning the Countertrade War* by Matt Schaffer (Wiley & Sons) is an excellent start. International trade magazines frequently have articles on the subject. *World Trade*, a monthly magazine published by World Trade Magazine, Inc., Irvine, California, concentrates on smaller companies and frequently runs articles on countertrade experiences.

Probably the best and the fastest way to gain access to world traders who specialize in disposing of goods acquired in countertrade transactions is to get involved in one of the countertrade associations. Although only a few have been formed in the United States, more are definitely on the way. The biggest ones are the Defense Industries Offset Association (obviously run by large defense contractors) and the American Countertrade Association for non-defense companies. Some export trading company trade associations can also be helpful.

Marketing and Fee Setting

The method for soliciting countertrade clients overseas is no different from the normal international marketing techniques described in Chapter 7. Marketing in the United States is more difficult. Again, contacts made through trade associations are a good beginning. City and state international trade groups are also fertile territory. Referrals from the international departments of money center and major regional banks work well, as do referrals from executives of foreign banks with headquarters in the United States.

Fees for countertrade engagements are normally based on hourly rates. Two to three times the normal billing rate for domestic work is not unusual. If an engagement requires monitoring a transaction for several years, a monthly retainer should be used with additional hourly billings for special negotiating, recruiting, or training work.

COUNTRY EVALUATION ENGAGEMENTS

The third rapidly growing segment of the international finance and administration market involves assisting clients to choose the appropriate country or region to trade in and then determining the tax, legal, administrative, and operating hazards clients will face. Choosing an appropriate country or region is part of the strategic planning process. As described in Chapter 6, the development of a company's mission leads to a determination of specific objectives to achieve this mission. Consultants help the board and top management focus on long-range strategies that meet these objectives. To the extent that they encompass global trade, consultants can assist in the analyses and evaluations of specific alternatives, including the choice of country or region to export to, import from, or in which to establish an operating presence.

Sources of Information

A wealth of written material provides market, trade barrier, and financial data covering every nation and region in the world. The Department of Commerce, industry trade associations, city and state economic development bureaus, international periodicals, and business books offer an abundance of choices for learning about and keeping continually updated on political, economic, and trade conditions around the globe.

Consultants who regularly digest this material should be in a position to present clients with a variety of factual options. Experience in the international sphere provides you with the background to interpret this data for clients and to assist in matching up the most likely choices with client objectives.

This may be as far as you have to go. If a client's objectives can be met merely by exporting to or importing from one or two countries, an analysis of data about those countries from readily available sources provides sufficient information to act on. On the other hand, if a client's objectives can best be achieved by establishing a physical presence in a foreign country (referred to as a foreign direct investment), then additional data will have to be gathered. This additional step is called a "country survey."

Country Survey

Country surveys give clients enough information to make tactical decisions about operating a facility in a specific country. They include data about local tax laws, legal and audit requirements, living conditions, trade barriers, labor and material availability, and a myriad of other details affecting the smooth transition into a new market.

A company may be in the export business for years without ever encountering the logistics of setting up a facility, managing a project, or otherwise making a direct investment in a foreign country. To attempt such a venture without a thorough grasp of the peculiar rules and regulations inherent in doing business in that country results in confusion and loss of profits. At worst, ignorance can doom the project to failure before it ever gets off the ground.

Consultants typically conduct country surveys in two distinct parts: the administrative segment, dealing with general and national policy matters, and a more detailed investigation relating to the client's specific project. Most of the administrative data can be obtained while still at home. Detailed operating information must be gathered on location.

The administrative survey covers:

- An analysis of the political/economic climate of the country
- Recommendations concerning alternative business structures for the foreign facility
- Audit, tax, legal and licensing rules
- Banking affiliation at home and in the host country
- Communications between the foreign location and the client's home office
- Selection of legal and audit professional advisors in the host country
- Personnel matters affecting travel to and from the foreign location
- Insurance coverage

A detailed investigation consists of:

- Enlisting interpreters in the host country
- An analysis of safety and security measures
- Host country and U.S. trade barriers that affect imports and exports
- U.S. and host country government subsidies

- Marketing practices, distribution, and controls in the foreign location
- Materials, supplies, and equipment availability and cost
- Host country labor and management resources and local labor laws
- Shipping and transport to, from, and within the host country
- Availability and reliability of electricity, fuel, and telephone service
- Living accommodations and health care for client personnel
- Education and social facilities for client personnel and families

Company personnel who seldom have the time or the wherewithal to perform either segment of the survey find consultants the least expensive and fastest way to get the job done. Very often country survey engagements lead directly to financial sourcing and negotiating. Occasionally they also lead to countertrade work.

In an effort to standardize the approach to country surveys, I have found the checklists in Figures 8–1 and 8–2 helpful. Clients appreciate an organized approach and this listing makes them feel comfortable that you have things under control.

Figure 8-1
CHECKLIST OF ADMINISTRATIVE DATA

Political/economic

1. U.S. and host country trade barriers to foreign investment, imports, and exports
2. Form of host country government—elected, monarchy, dictator, militant—and projected changes in the future
3. Explicit and implicit attitude toward the race, religion, or national origin of client personnel
4. Host country's major imports and exports

5. Economic indicators showing growth or decline in economic base
6. Controlled or free market
7. Ownership of host country businesses—private or government

Business Structure

1. Foreign business ownership laws
2. Requirements for local business partners—government or private
3. Laws governing percent ownership with local partner
4. Pros and cons of structuring the host country facility as a division or subsidiary of your client versus keeping it entirely separate

Audit, Tax, Legal, Licensing

1. Lists of correspondent law offices and accounting firms
2. Business licensing requirements
3. Recommendations for coping with local political graft
4. Unique laws affecting the race, religion, or national origin of client personnel
5. Work permit or visa restrictions
6. Compliance requirements for pertinent U.S. laws
7. Availability of assistance in host country legal matters
8. U.S. and host country audit and financial reporting requirements
9. Tax Information Exchange Agreement (TIEA) status of host country
10. Personal and corporate income tax rates and special tax provisions of host country
11. Tax or other incentives
12. Host country qualification for location of Foreign Sales Corporation

Banking

1. Listing of branch and correspondent banks and names of managers
2. Ability of client's U.S. bank to handle wire transfers, L/Cs, shipping document verification, currency conversion, and exchange arbitrage
3. Cost and timing of each of the bank's services
4. Bank reference letters and assurance of guarantees
5. Communications network with local U.S. bank
6. Participation in federal financing and assistance programs
7. English speaking branch managers
8. International communications systems employed

Communications

1. Stage of development of telephone service to and from the host country
2. Cost of telephone service and calls
3. AT & T or other telephone company international credit cards
4. Status of telex communications systems in the host country
5. Reliability of electric service and telephone service for computers
6. Courier companies serving host country
7. Pick up and delivery points for courier service and time interval for sending and receiving
8. Status of reliability and timing of mail service to and from the host country

Professional Advisors

1. List of government-connected lawyers to assist in dealing with federal bureaucracy
2. List of lawyers in host country that can do the same
3. Host country data from "Big Six" accounting firms

4. Trade association assistance
5. References from other foreign companies doing business in host country

Personnel

1. Names and addresses of employment agencies listing international managers
2. A passport for everyone
3. International drivers' licenses
4. Required and recommended vaccinations for everyone
5. List of English-speaking physicians in host country
6. Medical kits for everyone
7. U.S. bank letters of credit for financial emergencies
8. Company credit cards, preferably American Express and money center bank Visa or Mastercard
9. Airline schedules and fares

Insurance

1. Review of group health, life and accidental policies for overseas coverage
2. Comparison of rates from private carriers with FCIA for political and commercial risk
3. Company owned or leased foreign cars included in domestic policy, if possible
4. Short-term rental cars for temporary travelers

Figure 8-2
CHECKLIST OF DETAILED OPERATING DATA

General

1. Arrange for one or more interpreters to work with company personnel.

2. Notify American embassy, American Chamber of Commerce, and local police of the identity of each expatriate in the country and his/her purpose in being there.

3. Arrange for security guard protection of facility.

4. Determine specific import/export restrictions for material, equipment and products.

5. Open accounts with a local bank.

6. Make arrangements for permission to repatriate/convert currency.

7. Arrange with government officials for tax I.D., business license application, and other business permits.

Business

1. Contact local trading company about marketing restrictions and practices and arrange for distribution rights.

2. Talk with local Western firms about customary pricing structures.

3. Determine what formal government subsidies are available.

4. Make contact with local attorney.

5. Determine what materials, supplies, and equipment are necessary to start-up facility, where they will come from, and what import barriers exist.

6. Determine adequacy of labor base and management talent, including cost and availability.

7. Contact local labor broker for importing labor.

8. Arrange with local employment office to source management talent.

9. Collect data about ocean shipping and air freight out of country.

10. Negotiate arrangements with local trucking company for inland transport.

11. Determine licensing requirements and availability of power and water.

Personnel

1. Collect data about expatriate housing accommodations and food cost.

2. Investigate public transportation and leased auto availability and cost.

3. Accumulate brochures, cost information, and other data for family educational facilities.

4. Prepare collection of leisure time opportunities.

Consulting Qualifications

The primary qualification for performing country evaluations is a basic knowledge of where to obtain information. The book *Going Global: New Opportunities for Growing Companies to Compete in World Markets* includes an entire chapter describing sources of international information. Here is a recap of the most prominent and accessible sources:

1. Department of Commerce. Two sister agencies, the International Trade Administration (ITA) and the United States & Foreign Commercial Service (US&FCS), maintain mammoth computer data banks of information from nearly every country in the world. Hard copy or computer disc reports are easily obtainable at nominal fees covering trade and investment opportunities, markets for specific products and services, overseas buyers and representatives, financing, international trade exhibits, export documentation requirements, economic and demographic statistics, licensing, and seminars.

2. Overseas Business Reports (OBRs). OBRs identify economic, market, and product trends in specific regions of the world. Special reports can be obtained covering market size, distribution channels, forecasted market potential, business customs and practices, customer analyses, implicit and explicit trade barriers, competitive environment, specific trade contacts, and legal restrictions. Customized market research studies can also be obtained for a small fee.

3. Country desk officers. Country desk officers in ITAs International Economic Policy unit maintain up-to-date information by country including regulations, tariffs, economic and political developments, business practices, trade data and trends, market size, and market growth.

4. Small Business Administration. Some SBA offices counsel companies starting out in global trade about local regulations and opportunities. Most offices, however, are ill-equipped to offer substantive information.

5. State and city commissions. Nearly every state and large city maintain active trade commissions to foster exporting business. Most provide counseling services, information gathering departments, federal export coordination, technical assistance, and financial advice.

6. Private sector. Universities, "Big Six" accounting firms, and money center banks all produce pamphlets and newsletters on current international trade developments. In addition to *The Economist* magazine, which should be "must" reading, four publication are worth getting:

- *Background News* from the Bureau of Public Affairs, Department of State
- *Operational Information on Proposed Projects* from the Asian Development Bank
- *United Nations Development Business*, included in the Business Edition of the Development Forum
- *International Business Outlook* from the World Bank

7. Foreign chambers of commerce. Over forty countries maintain chamber of commerce offices in the United States. Most will supply commercial and economic information on request.

Fee Structures and Marketing

Fees are usually based on hourly rates, except when you travel overseas on behalf of the client. Then weekly or monthly flat fees should be used. Hourly rates run the same as all international work, about two to three times those charged for domestic engagements. For extended engagements, monthly retainers are a good idea, especially for smaller clients. Consultants seldom go after clients specifically for country evaluation engagements. Evaluation work takes place after advising a client about entering or expanding in international trade. Consequently, marketing efforts should be directed to obtaining full finance and administration engagements rather than merely country evaluations.

CONSULTING ORGANIZATION AND SCOPE CONTRACTS

With the exception of overseas travel, much of the work on international finance and administration jobs can be accomplished from your office, either by telephone, data base access, fax, or mail. Most clients will be from your country of origin.

Although financial institutions and countertrade traders are sourced globally, much of the search and original contact work can be done at home. Foreign travel is necessary to arrange and negotiate the final contract, but that is a minor time segment of the entire engagement. Analogous circumstances apply to country evaluations.

As opposed to other segments of international consulting, the finance and administration niche is ideal for sole practitioners. Handling two or three clients simultaneously normally presents little difficulty. The short time spans required for overseas work allow consortium associates to easily cover for you. It does help to have one administrative person in the office, however. The volume of phone calls, fax messages, computer data transfers, and mail requests can be overwhelming. The cost of an administrative person is more than compensated for by the high fees that can be charged.

This is one market niche that requires an efficient telecommunications setup and ready access to several global computer data bases. Government data, financing sources, trading customers, government agencies, project bids, market and competitive statistics, and data bases with a variety of other information can be accessed directly in your office. If you don't have administrative assistance, however, it doesn't take long to be overwhelmed with hard copy reports.

Characteristically, engagements in this market niche tend to bring in repeat business. By efficiently handling the financing or administration of a foreign project you will invariably get additional work either from the client's home office or from the foreign location. The scarcity of qualified international consultants specializing in finance and administration makes supply far less than demand. As a result, references from satisfied clients should net more business than you can handle.

Scope contracts are difficult to write for finance and administration engagements because very often the client can't define precisely what role you will play. What begins as a financing assignment often ends with countertrade. Country evaluations nearly always follow from financing or countertrade engagements, assuming the client plans to locate abroad.

The most feasible type of scope contract is open-ended. That is, you contract to assist in sourcing financing, for example, but leave the precise scope broad enough to include other activities as they come up. If you plan to use different fee structures for different types of work assignments, the range and possible variations should be spelled out. To retain good client relations for repeat business it's important to define all possibilities right in the beginning.

9 *Troubled Company Market*

Troubled companies have always needed help. In the past four years, however, several factors combined to increase dramatically the complexity of their problems as well as the number of companies in financial difficulty. Overextended banks and other lending institutions, eager to strike while the iron was hot, made loans without regard to the future cash generating ability of borrowers. Forced by regulators to face up to deteriorating balance sheets, they stopped lending and began calling outstanding loans from companies already facing cash shortfalls.

As early as mid-1989 sections of the country fell into a deep recession, even though government economists wouldn't recognize it until eighteen months later. Blinded by the glory days of easy credit and consumer spending sprees, companies with overstocked inventories and excess personnel recognized too late the inherent weaknesses in the economy. In the midst of these internal aberrations, oil prices skyrocketed, consumer confidence ebbed, banks continued to tighten credit, and the federal government stood meekly by, strangled by political confusion.

These detrimental economic circumstances forced bankruptcy rates to double each year since 1987. Liquidation auctions dotted the landscape. More than 200 commercial banks failed every year. The entire savings and loan industry fell into disarray with hundreds of banks now managed by federal regulators. Foreign buyers bailed out a small number of companies, and a few banks, by acquiring them for a song, but the majority that remain in business are in serious jeopardy. They need all the help they can get and consultants can provide it.

Two major obstacles prevent capable consultants from entering this exploding market niche. First, working with business owners and managers of companies that have failed or that are on the brink of failure seems to bring unsavory connotations. Consultants fear that becoming associated with troubled clients somehow tarnishes their reputation for the glamour jobs.

To an extent the argument holds water. Working with managements of distressed companies can be a disheartening experience. It certainly isn't as easy as performing strategic planning engagements for profitable growth companies or as exciting as M & A work. Consulting to troubled companies is hard work, time consuming, bruising, and, to a large extent, unappreciated.

On the flip side, consultants who have ventured into this market niche find more business than they can handle. I have never met one whose reputation was tarnished or who was prevented from handling other, more socially acceptable engagements.

Several other advantages also accrue. Getting a company back on its feet can be an extremely rewarding personal accomplishment. The work is dynamic, ever-changing, and never boring. It is creative. No two assignments follow the same path. No one has come up with the "right" way to handle one of these engagements. And when you do save a company, continuing engagements always follow for extended periods.

The second reason consultants shy away from this market is the belief that distressed companies cannot afford to pay for consulting services. Again, to some extent this is also true. Companies in trouble with their banks are always short of cash. No cash reserves sit buried in obscure accounts. There certainly isn't enough cash to pay for all the help they need.

On the other hand, just as companies filing under Chapter 11 scrape together enough cash for outlandish attorney's fees, troubled companies somehow find enough to pay for relatively short-term consulting help. In addition, for those assignments that stretch on for months, or even years, substantial equity shares can more than offset the dearth of cash fees.

A close consulting friend specializes in this market. He earns enough cash fees to sustain a very comfortable standard of living. On top of that, he has taken equity shares in five companies as partial payment for consulting work. One of those companies recently went public and my friend netted a cool $2 million for his shares!

SPECIAL TERMINOLOGY

Three broad classifications define troubled company consulting: turn-arounds, workouts, and liquidations. Each of the three is dramatically different from the others, except that they all deal with companies in financial trouble.

A turnaround engagement presupposes that by implementing sound management practices the company can be made profitable in a relatively short period of time.

A workout engagement typically occurs shortly before and immediately after a company files for protection under Chapter 11 of the Bankruptcy Code.

A liquidation is self-explanatory, involving the disposition of company assets and a termination of operations. Clearly, one type of engagement can lead to the other. Unsuccessful turnarounds become workouts. Unsuccessful workouts turn into liquidations.

Consultants, as well as lenders, have coined the phrase "crisis management" to define the type of activities performed for these clients. Certainly, each of the three categories can be a crisis, and certainly managerial talents are required for the consultant to be successful.

Nevertheless, the term has a sour ring to it and connotes brink-manship. In reality, at least for turnarounds and workouts, a consultant's main task is to bring the company into a profitable mode, which is a positive result. The terms "turnaround," "workout," and "liquidation" adequately describe each type of engagement and will be used from here on.

TURNAROUNDS

Turnaround specialists are like doctors, except instead of treating sick people they treat sick companies. If the diagnosis is correct the prescribed cure usually works and the patient heals. Medical success or failure turns on making the proper diagnosis. Exactly the same condition exists in turnaround work. If a consultant correctly diagnoses the client's problems, corrective actions can usually save the company. The wrong diagnosis nearly always kills.

Another analogy also holds. In medicine, some diseases come on quickly, without warning. Most, however, display symptoms early on. If the doctor catches a patient in the early stages, most illnesses can be cured. Waiting too long brings opposite results.

Occasionally companies also acquire illnesses quickly, without warning: a flood, fire, massive lawsuit, labor strike, IRS action, and a few other conditions make a company very ill, very fast. In most cases, however, sick companies exhibit symptoms long before circumstances become acute. If a consultant can get in the door when the symptoms are still manageable, the turnaround can be accomplished in short order with relatively little pain. Waiting until the end is near often requires massive surgery.

Size and Type of Client

Turnaround clients come in all sizes, in all industries, and in all locations. Of course when very large corporations get sick chances are high that the federal government will step in to bail them out without consulting help, such as happened with Continental Bank, Lockheed Corporation, and the S & Ls.

Although turnaround clients can be publicly owned or privately held, most sole practitioners or small firm turnaround consultants remain blocked by the large banks, law firms, and federal government from actively participating in very large corporate turnarounds, or workouts and liquidations for that matter. Therefore, this chapter focuses on working for clients in the small to mid-size range.

Turnaround Work

Several types of symptoms cause a company to become ill. A consultant's first job is to diagnose the illness. The next stage defines corrective action steps. Far and away the most common circumstance causing financial disability is an unmanageable debt load. Sound balance sheet principles have been given short shrift. The matchup of short-term debt for short-term purposes and long-term debt for long-term purposes has been violated.

With an easy credit environment and no strategic plan, companies often find themselves in hot water with a bank even before business turns sour. Using borrowed money to overstock inventory, hire excess personnel, purchase unnecessary hard assets, and pay unwarranted salaries and bonuses invariably results in cash shortfalls when it's time to pay back the loans.

Some of the other common ailments driving a company to financial turmoil are:

- Intensification of competition, either from foreign firms or from new entrants to the market
- Technological change that obsoletes products
- Macroeconomic swings in the national economy
- Industry aberrations resulting in substitute products
- Federal government interference in industry or company standards and practices
- Excess cash withdrawals by the business owner
- Court-decreed judgments

When hiring a consultant to effect a cure, clients hardly ever define the specific nature of the assignment. Scope contracts are very imprecise, often incorporating very clear "best effort" clauses. Certainly, consultants cannot guarantee results in this type of engagement.

The type of work varies all over the lot. In extreme cases, consultants are called upon to run the company for an interim period. In other cases they manage a specific function, such as the controller's department or the production operation. In other cases, a complete restructuring is called for. Consultants source and negotiate new financing and negotiate settlements with current lenders.

Many engagements require consultants to actively recruit top management personnel, including the CEO. Not infrequently, they propose and implement the sale of a division, product line, subsidiary, or even the entire company. In other cases, they perform the search and negotiation for new equity money. In one engagement, I recommended an offensive strategy and ended up sourcing, financing, and negotiating two business acquisitions for the client.

No commonality exists between tactical approaches to turn-around engagements. Each patient requires a distinct approach to cure its ills. If there is any similarity between engagements, it is to keep lenders at bay while trying to turn the client around.

Regardless of what specific actions consultants get called upon to implement, the starting point in any turnaround engagement is a planning session with the business owner or CEO. This planning session addresses two issues: the short-term steps necessary to salvage the company, and the longer-range tactical moves to get the company back on its feet. It takes months to resolve planning issues in profitable companies. With turnarounds, plans must be conceived in days.

The primary short-term objective must be to increase the amount of discretionary cash available for debt service payments. Survival tactics to achieve this typically consist of steps to:

1. Reduce personnel costs.
2. Hasten receivables collections.
3. Eliminate travel, entertainment, and other non-essential expenses.
4. Reduce purchases of materials and supplies.
5. Renegotiate leases.
6. Raise selling prices.
7. Sell off old inventory.
8. Sell non-critical equipment, machinery, vehicles, and real estate.
9. Reduce selling expenses.

The main long-term objective (and long-term in turnaround situations means one to two years) is to reshape the organization, product lines, asset base, and debt structure to enable the company to generate profits. Typical long-term moves include steps to:

1. Prune low-profit product lines.
2. Prioritize customer mix.

3. Recruit capable managers.
4. Renegotiate short-term to long-term debt.
5. Bring additional equity into the business.
6. Effect a sale/leaseback of hard assets.
7. Develop an impact advertising program.
8. Implement a non-cash employee incentive program.
9. Put in new control systems.
10. Borrow from customers/vendors.

If client managers had the ability and will to implement these steps they would do so and consultants would not be necessary. However, since the company is in a turnaround position, this has not happened. Therefore, consultants must carry the ball. Turnaround consulting requires hands-on management, not advice. Consultants must have management authority to make survival decisions. They also have the responsibility to persuade top management that their way works and is the only way to survive. And, of course, they have the responsibility to keep secured lenders informed about what they are doing.

Fee Structure

Fees for turnarounds are quite varied, depending on the client's cash position and the willingness of secured lenders to allow the client to pay consultants in lieu of meeting debt service obligations. Turnaround jobs normally command standard hourly billing rates. Successful engagements are certainly worth more, but because of cash problems, clients can seldom pay more.

One alternative might be to take an equity share in the company in exchange for keeping hourly rates to a minimum. Another, less severe, measure grants the consultant options to purchase an equity share at a later date at a bargain basement price. If the turnaround works, you have a good investment. If it doesn't, you lose only the excess fees that could not be billed anyway.

Since turnarounds are management engagements, extending for long periods of time, retainers or advance payments become absolutely essential. Turnaround companies are always short of cash.

Therefore, it's safer to demand weekly advance payments rather than monthly or quarterly retainers.

WORKOUTS

Workout engagements represent the next step down the ladder from turnarounds. By the time a company reaches the workout stage secured and unsecured creditors are pounding on the door. Management personnel have become disheartened. The business owner or CEO has for all practical purposes given up. Customers reduce order rates. Suppliers refuse to ship on credit.

Whereas the probability of success in a turnaround normally reaches 60 to 70 percent, successful workouts run about 30 percent. In other words, chance are high you will not be successful in implementing a workout program. This changes the approach to performing the job, to billing procedures, and, to a lesser extent, the qualifications a consultant should possess.

Workouts occur when a company approaches the doors of bankruptcy as well as when it has already filed under Chapter 11. Obviously, better results can be achieved by coming in before the filing. At least then you have some flexibility to implement programs without concurrence from the court and creditor committee. Once under the jurisdiction of the bankruptcy court, a company's options become substantially more limited.

Workout Engagements

The starting point in a workout, just as with a turnaround, is a planning session with the business owner or CEO. In workouts, however, there isn't time for long-range planning. Now immediate action must be taken and the planning session focuses on a program to bring extra cash into the business in the very short-term, next week and next month. The consulting approach can best be described as "fire and fall back." The precision of implementing changes is less important than the implementation itself.

Typically, workout clients have far too much inventory, too many people on the payroll, the owner or CEO is drawing too much compensation, and no one controls expenses. Cash management is non-existent. This bleeding must first be stopped before improvements can be implemented. Most business owners or CEOs won't voluntarily grant you authority to take the necessary actions. Leverage must be applied. Lending institutions provide the leverage.

Although banks of any type are always concerned about conflict of interest and therefore do not dare issue management orders, they can and do exert a substantial amount of indirect pressure. For example, "We will foreclose on the loan if you don't get the company straightened out in two months. Here is a consultant with the ability to do the job. The choice is yours!" Such a clear message usually penetrates and you get the authority.

Except in unusual circumstances consultants should implement all of the following actions within the first month:

1. Trim payroll by 20 percent.
2. Transfer part or all of the cost of employee benefit programs to employees.
3. Raise selling prices 30 to 50 percent.
4. Cut the owner's or CEO's salary in half.
5. Sell excess inventory at distress prices.
6. Implement stringent cash management procedures, expense controls, and purchasing budgets.
7. Negotiate with vendors for extended payment terms of old accounts.

Once the bleeding stops, other tactics can be put in place.

1. Implement a tough receivables collections program, offering discounts for early payment if necessary.
2. Eliminate all travel except for sales personnel.
3. Put a lid on all entertainment and other superfluous expenses.
4. Implement a purchasing budget for "just in time" deliveries.
5. Renegotiate leases for lower monthly payments.
6. Raise selling prices a second time.
7. Sell non-critical equipment, machinery, vehicles, and real estate.
8. Transfer all salaried sales personnel to commissions.

9. Implement a non-cash employee incentive program.
10. Bring in equity cash by selling part of the company, perhaps to employees through an Employee Stock Ownership Plan (ESOP).

If the client begins to show improvement from these action steps and cash flow loosens a bit, you can begin to assist in the implementation of the balance of the turnaround tactics.

Bankruptcy Workouts

Workout engagements leading to the filing of a bankruptcy proceeding under Chapter 11, or those for clients already in Chapter 11, take on a different tone. If called in early enough, you can help structure insiders' compensation during the ninety days preceding the filing to reduce the probability of preference payment suits. Tactics can also be developed for threatening unsecured creditors with a bankruptcy filing as leverage for restructuring deferred payments schedules.

Frequently the greatest service consultants render during the pre-petition period is to meet with suppliers, employee groups, other unsecured creditors, and legal counsel to reach agreement on deferred payments. If successful, such agreements might forestall a bankruptcy filing and allow the client some breathing space. It's also important to meet with secured creditors during this period. Try to convert short-term debt to long-term notes, or get approval for deferred principle and/or interest payments on term loans. On more than one occasion consultants have helped clients avoid bankruptcy by being tough with bankers during this period.

Once clients file under Chapter 11, they must get approval from the court to hire consultants. It is usually granted. The same operating tactics described for pre-petition workouts apply during the reorganization period. In addition, consultants are frequently called upon to meet with a creditor committee to structure a reorganization plan.

Throughout the entire process, both before and after the client files for bankruptcy protection, consultants must be extremely careful to avoid liability for preference payments and to prevent conflicts of interest from arising. The only solution is to become intimately familiar with the rules and regulations of the federal Bankruptcy Code. A definitive scope contract replete with hold harmless clauses provides additional protection but is not foolproof. If a third party sues you and the client is broke, hold harmless clauses won't do much good.

Fee Structure

Since workout clients are in worse shape than turnarounds, the likelihood of billing fees in excess of normal is very remote. Most workouts are billed at the standard rate for hours worked. Weekly advance payments must be used to avoid delinquencies. Also, secured creditors should approve of the fee structure prior to taking on the engagement. After filing Chapter 11, the court must approve fees and it becomes very difficult to get advance payments.

LIQUIDATIONS

When secured creditors see no hope of saving a company they foreclose, hoping to recoup their loans by selling business assets. If a client has already filed Chapter 11, and the court cannot be convinced that a reorganization plan is feasible, it can convert the filing to a Chapter 7 liquidation under the supervision of a court-appointed trustee. Prior to filing for bankruptcy protection, unsecured creditors can force the company into a Chapter 7 liquidation. Consultants play an important role in all of these cases.

The major task for consultants in liquidation engagements is to assist creditors and/or a trustee to arrange for the winding down of a company's business and the liquidation of its assets. By this stage the business owner or CEO has no authority over the proceedings and consultants take their direction from external parties.

A secured creditor or a trustee might appoint a consulting firm to manage the company during the wind down. This involves terminating employees, selling supplies and loose inventory, collecting from customers, and paying bills. It might also involve negotiating settlements with suppliers and other parties with claims against the company. Sometimes you are asked to assist an accountant in filing the final tax returns. A variety of tasks must be accomplished before the doors finally close and at this stage secured creditors and bankruptcy courts usually don't trust the owner or the company's managers to do the job.

If assets are to be sold at an auction, arrangements must be made with an auctioneer and a proper location selected. Consultants are frequently called upon to arrange both. Consultants can also make sure the company complies with bulk sales laws. Once the assets are sold, trustees often look to consultants to assist in the distribution of proceeds to creditors.

Fee Structure

Liquidation engagements normally command flat fees for the entire project. With secured creditor approval consultants can obtain partial payments in advance, say one-third, with another one-third when partially completed and the balance at the end of the liquidation. Bankruptcy lawyers work this way and courts and secured creditors will usually go along with it for consultants. The danger in flat fees, of course, is that you must estimate the right amount of hours or you can lose your shirt. Most consultants jack their fees up high enough to take care of any contingency.

In a bankruptcy liquidation, court-approved consulting fees are considered "administrative expenses" and paid prior to disbursing auction proceeds to creditors.

Theoretically, consultants work for the liquidating company. Pragmatically, however, either secured creditors, the creditors' committee, or the trustee actually engages consulting firms. A definitive scope agreement must be executed with the company, but third parties stand behind it.

CONSULTING QUALIFICATIONS

No technical expertise is required for consulting to troubled companies other than a gutsy personality, a strong constitution, and a thorough grasp of federal bankruptcy laws as well as of state and federal debtor/creditor laws. You don't need to be a lawyer. Several books are available that provide detailed explanations of salient provisions and that's enough for a start. As you get involved in these engagements it doesn't take long to pick up legal nuances.

Hard-core experience, either as an employee in a troubled company or by owning one yourself, is invaluable background. Managing troubled companies takes a radically different approach than running a profitable, healthy business. Short-term objectives take precedence over long-term improvements. Cash shortfalls dictate creative solutions to daily operating problems. Poor employee morale forces much closer management attention to details, requiring time and effort that would be better applied to getting the company redirected and to resolving disputes with banks and other creditors. Lawsuits come out of the woodwork.

Managing means getting intimately involved in day-to-day events and making spot decisions. Seldom, if ever, can you delegate either management authority or responsibility in a troubled company. The boss must be an active participant in everything.

Because troubled companies need this short-term, hands-on approach to management, consultants specializing in this niche must have substantial general management background. They must be proficient in managing activities in all functions of the business: sales, production, accounting, systems, customer services, advertising, engineering, and human relations. This background can only come from experience, not classrooms, seminars, or books.

Consultants must also have strong negotiating abilities. A large part of troubled company consulting involves negotiating with banks, suppliers, unions, the IRS, individual employees, and customers. There is no time for lengthy debates. Negotiations must be swift and to the point. However, leveraging the threat of bankruptcy usually gives you the edge.

Most consultants who do well in this specialty niche seem to have the following background and personal characteristics:

Experiential Background

1. Experience in management position of one or more troubled companies

2. Involvement in at least one lawsuit, either as plaintiff, defendant, as advisor to one or the other, or as an expert witness

3. Intense exposure to business finance, cost accounting, contract negotiations and administration, and personnel evaluations

4. General management responsibilities in a small or mid-size company
5. Thorough grasp of financial statements and how the numbers interrelate
6. Working relationships with public accountants, bankers, and lawyers

Personal Characteristics

1. Authoritative demeanor to elicit confidence
2. Outward-going personality with excellent relationship skills
3. Persuasive and logical thought processes to make snap decisions
4. Professional appearance for meetings with bankers, customers, and suppliers, and for court appearances
5. Freedom to travel for extended periods
6. Honesty and straightforwardness with credentials to prove it
7. GUTSY!

It's probably not a good idea to pursue this specialty without at least most of these credentials. Troubled company consulting is difficult enough even with the right background and personal traits. It can be a nightmare without them.

COMPETITION

Competition in this specialty is nationwide. The market is not regionalized: it spans the country. Fortunately, even with national coverage, few consultants choose this niche. Competition is probably less nationwide than in any other consulting market. And with the number of potential clients shooting through the roof, plenty of business should be available for years to come.

Most of the competition that does exist comes from banks and law firms, with small but growing participation by specialized departments in the "Big Six" accounting firms. Because of the rise in bankruptcies and the concern over non-performing loans, many banks have formed their own workout departments. Most are staffed with ex-loan officers with little management knowledge and virtually no experience in turnarounds. Although bank workout departments can be bothersome, their lack of management expertise precludes serious long-term competition. They offer virtually no competition for turnaround engagements.

Law firms specializing in bankruptcies occasionally try to compete in Chapter 11 workouts and Chapter 7 liquidations. Most do not want to dirty their hands with detailed operating problems, however, and their effect in the total market remains negligible. Also smart lawyers are very cognizant of conflict of interest accusations. They would rather stick with their law books and courts than get involved in managing a business.

The strongest long-term competition will probably come from the "Big Six" accounting firms. As Andersen Consulting stretches to control more esoteric markets, we can expect further competition in the troubled company niche as well. Because of the larger firms' cumbersome bureaucratic structures, however, their flexibility and ability to respond quickly remains limited. Chances are good that as they evolve in this niche they will concentrate on large corporate clients rather than on smaller ones, just as they do in other markets.

MARKETING

As previously stated, turnarounds, workouts, and liquidations all require different approaches to performing the work. Turnaround assignments emphasize solving operating problems and getting the company back up and running profitably again.

Workouts actually break into two spheres: before filing Chapter 11 and reorganization efforts after filing. Tactics applied to pre-petition workouts concentrate on very short-term moves to increase cash. Reorganization work involves negotiating settlements with creditors and coordinating with the courts.

Liquidations are short-lived assignments concerned solely with disposing of business assets and winding down a company's affairs. As production efforts vary with each segment, so do marketing approaches.

Turnarounds

Troubled companies classified as turnarounds continue to operate fairly independent of lender interference. Management might be proficient in some areas and lacking in others. A consultant's role is to first diagnose the illness and then prescribe appropriate cures.

Turnaround marketing efforts should be directed toward the business owner or CEO. Because of the psychology of failure associated with troubled companies and the stigma that accompanies perceived failure, owners and managers do not like to broadcast their problems. Employees, suppliers, customers and lenders might have an inkling that something is amiss but management does not want to rock the boat by acknowledging their suspicions. For this reason, discretion plays a major role in marketing to turnarounds.

The same hesitancy by company management to admit financial difficulties prevents consultants from effectively using the referral route. Theoretically at least, lenders, customers, and suppliers are not supposed to know that the company is in trouble.

A formal advertising campaign is useless, for exactly the same reasons. No prospective client wants to reveal financial aberrations to a stranger. Direct mail, TV and radio spots, and other direct advertising ploys fall flat.

Three avenues work exceptionally well for getting turnaround clients: discreet public awareness campaigns, authorship of books and articles, and referrals from public accounting firms. One of the best ways to make the public aware of your expertise is to appear as a speaker or panelist at seminars or conferences directed toward business owners and top management. The agenda might include taxes, business plans, strategic planning, cash management, financing options, or any number of other related topics. It's easy to work comments and suggestions applicable to troubled companies into your presentation. That's enough of a lead to encourage executives to look you up after the seminar or conference ends.

Authorship is another indirect way to establish your authority in the field. Many consultants with writing ability find this an excellent way to introduce themselves without an actual appearance. Whether you write a book or articles for trade periodicals, topics should revolve around methods for turning a company around. If your publisher's marketing organization knows how to sell, you should get more business than you can handle.

Referrals from small and mid-size public accounting firms are usually the fastest way to get turnaround clients. All CPAs have clients in trouble. They don't want to take the assignment themselves fearing a conflict of interest. A casual suggestion that a client should give you a call often works wonders. Turnaround consultants have good contacts with these professional firms usually don't have to go any further to get business.

Workouts

Getting workout clients is a different matter entirely. Here lenders are the dominant force. Banks, finance companies, the SBA, and other lenders take a proprietary interest in getting their customers out of the soup. With the exception of finance companies, lenders would much rather help a customer clean up its problems than be forced to foreclose.

Workout consultants spend 90 percent of their marketing effort on lenders, mainly banks and local SBA offices. Getting started in this specialty usually requires a great many cold calls on bank officers responsible for non-performing loans. It won't do any good to call on loan officers. You must get to the people handling non-performing loans.

Even banks with in-house workout departments often use consultants if they see any chance of the customer being righted. Workout departments notwithstanding, banks cannot afford to become involved in management decisions. If new or better management is the answer they use consultants.

Nearly every bank that makes commercial loans maintains a list of workout consultants. When the bank decides a customer needs help, it offers the list along with discreet suggestions for the best choice. Cold calls and constant follow-up get your name on the list. Those banks with which you have established a good relationship will be apt to discreetly recommend your firm over others. Constant calling, meaningful follow-up, and a little romancing generally get bankers on your side. The hardest part of this process is getting to the right person in the bank. It takes perseverance.

Liquidations

The same lenders that deserve marketing attention for workouts provide the contacts for liquidations. In some cases, after foreclosure, a bank might hire consultants directly to handle the liquidation. More often, however, they force the liquidating company to execute the contract.

Finance companies are another good source for liquidation engagements. Finance companies are also fully capable of managing auctions. They continually work with auctioneers and know exactly how, when, and where to sell the assets. Little opportunity exists for consultants to break this loop. However, winding down a company's affairs is another matter.

Although most finance companies (asset-based lenders) have qualified people on their staffs to manage workouts, they would rather stay clear of conflict of interest charges and turn the business wrap-up phase over to consultants. This may not be a very large part of the total liquidation effort but it must be done, and the engagements are usually quite short.

Bankruptcy lawyers offer another possibility for getting liquidation work. If a company is already in Chapter 7, a court-appointed trustee has the responsibility for ending the business. Bankruptcy lawyers always get involved. The bankruptcy field has a very close-knit group of participants. Everyone knows everyone else: lawyers, judges, and trustees. Although approaching judges is dangerous, letting bankruptcy lawyers know of your credentials and desire to handle liquidations frequently brings substantial business. They might get your firm appointed as trustee. More likely, however, they convince the trustee to hire you to do the dirty work of the liquidation.

CONSULTING ORGANIZATION

Most consulting engagements to troubled companies extend for many months, even years. Turnarounds can take consultants to distant divisions or subsidiaries. Workouts might involve traveling to suppliers and customers' locations. Even liquidations frequently occur in remote areas. Since troubled company consulting is a national market, not local or regional, consultants in this field must be prepared to be away from the office, often at great distances, for extended periods. As in other far-flung consulting markets, this creates a nightmare without a properly organized office.

Although some troubled company consultants remain sole practitioners, the onslaught of new business over the next decade dictates organizing as a partnership. Under certain circumstances consortiums and networks work for short-term exigencies but over the long-haul formal partnerships remain the only logical answer.

It's one thing to spend a month on a systems project at a client's site ten miles away. Managing a turnaround across the country for six to nine months presents quite a different set of organizational problems. In addition, because turnarounds and workouts normally entail a mix of management disciplines, it's entirely possible to come across problems that you do not have the capability of solving. A partner with those skills can save the day.

When I started in turnaround consulting I tried to do it as a sole practitioner. The first two assignments were local, and although they both extended for several months, my background was sufficient to resolve the client's management and banking problems. The third engagement took me to Los Angeles (my office was in Philadelphia). It began as a turnaround and ended as a voluntary liquidation.

The turning point revolved around a lawsuit claiming technical failure of my client's product. Without an engineering background I was totally lost and could offer no help in resolving the issue. When the engagement ended I promptly set about locating a partner with an engineering background, vowing never again to be caught with my pants down.

With more and more small and mid-size companies facing global markets, cross-border financing, technological explosions, and staggering changes in resource allocations, the next decade portends an escalating number of troubled companies with increasingly complex problems. Consultants wishing to take advantage of this burgeoning market need to get their organizations in place and management skills honed. The earlier that consultants with varying technical and management skills form partnerships and get a working, bionic office in place, the greater their probability of success.

Larger, multi-partner firms may choose to set up a separate department to handle troubled company engagements. Because the work involves general management skills, one partner should be in charge. Staff personnel can certainly help perform analytical tasks and systems evaluations but a partner must be on the premises to supervise them. This is excellent training for roles in future general management engagements.

Going this route normally involves a segregation of office functions as well as of staff. Since discretion is the by-word and confidentiality an absolute necessity, the fewer lower-level personnel involved the better.

On the other hand, the problem of professional liability often dissuades mid-size firms from branching out into this area. The likelihood of lawsuits is higher in this specialty than in most other types of engagements. Angry creditors and recalcitrant banks tend to look to the consulting firm as a scapegoat when they fail with the client. Normal liability insurance covers most cases, but with too many people engaged in this work premiums get expensive.

It seems inevitable that eventually other consultants will catch on to this lucrative field. They will see the market for what it is, a sizzling opportunity to cash in. They will also eventually understand that their reputations as reliable, capable management consultants will not be tarnished by taking on clients in financial trouble. Competition is bound to increase significantly. Consultants with the foresight and determination to get in early will be firmly established and capable of weathering any competitive storm. Those who linger stand to miss an outstanding opportunity.

REPEAT BUSINESS

One of the arguments advanced against concentrating in the troubled company market is that these engagements are short-lived, one-shot assignments without the likelihood of repeat business. Nothing could be further from the truth. While it is true that not all turnarounds work and many end up as liquidations, many more are successful. When a consultant is instrumental in turning a losing company into a winner repeat business never stops.

A good example of this occurred to a consulting associate who decided to bite the bullet and take a turnaround engagement. Harry was an ex-General Electric manager who turned to consulting after being laid off. He struggled for four years trying to build his consulting business when he landed the turnaround job. The manufacturing client was small, with annual sales of about $13 million. Its debt-ridden balance sheet proved that it was only steps away from bankruptcy, but the product lines were solid and the company had an outstanding reputation in the industry.

Harry worked the turnaround for thirteen months, finally breaking the banking logjam and freeing up sufficient cash for the client to introduce some new products. He refused the business owner's offer of the presidency, citing a desire to remain independent. Over the succeeding four years, the client hired Harry to install a computer system, to help the company structure an export program, and to reorganize the management team. In early 1991, Harry was working on a long-range strategic plan with the same company.

Repeat business comes from successful turnarounds and workouts more frequently than from practically any other specialty. The perception that troubled company engagements are one-shot jobs is a myth and should not deter serious consideration of this growing market.

10 Small Business Market

The entrepreneurial spirit is alive and well. Thousands of new businesses start-up every year. Department of Commerce statistics indicate a continuing growth over the foreseeable future. Furthermore, shifting socioeconomic conditions support the conclusion that the trend will not only continue but will escalate over the next decade.

As immigrants from East Asia, Mexico, Latin America, Eastern Europe, and the Middle East continue to flock to America's shores, language barriers, cultural differences, and skills inappropriate for American industry encourage these emigrés to try the entrepreneurial trail. Burgeoning ethnic neighborhoods supported by their own shops and service businesses in most large cities and many smaller towns prove that the trend is accelerating.

Executives, managers, and first line employees from every conceivable industry continue to suffer from "pink slip Friday." Disillusioned with corporate life, many try their hand at their own business. Young people, unable or unwilling to spend a small fortune on a college education shun low-paying menial jobs to become entrepreneurs. College graduates unable to locate the right job or unwilling to succumb to corporate platitudes venture out on their own. As long as entrepreneurial opportunities remain open, which they probably will indefinitely, there should be plenty of takers.

At the same time, the escalating annual rate of small business failures is a sure sign that help is needed. Very few business owners have concrete experience that combines marketing, production, finance, personnel management, taxes, accounting, application engineering, and quality assurance. Most have training in one or two areas, but seldom in all the disciplines necessary to run a business successfully. Bankers, lawyers, public accountants, SBA officials, friends, neighbors, and relatives all want to help, but few have the time, resources or experience to make much difference.

This creates enormous opportunities for consultants willing and able to service these small businesses. However, many smaller consulting firms and sole practitioners who, with their low overhead, could make a good living in this niche market, shun small business clients, citing low hourly rates and lack of future growth. This is a big mistake. In the beginning, it is true that small start-up businesses cannot afford $200 or even $100 hourly rates for extended periods. But with the right guidance many soon justify a reasonable rate for services they can't get elsewhere.

The "Big Six" accounting firms recognized this several years ago and implemented special departments specifically oriented to servicing small clients. They started with tax return preparation and lender compliance audits. Soon they branched out into general consulting work.

These strong competitors still operate in the small business market and get reasonable fees for their efforts, averaging around $125 an hour in larger cities. Many small business owners, however, and especially those just starting up, are frightened by the thought of engaging big firms. Those in smaller towns or rural communities don't even have the option of using the "Big Six." Smaller consulting firms and sole practitioners fill the gap in both instances.

Several characteristics of the small business market offer unusual opportunities for new consultants just getting started. Small businesses are all local, which eliminates travel time. Much of the work can be performed without ever leaving your office. Engagements are relatively unsophisticated, which allows time to learn the consulting business. Marketing small business clients is easier than most other market niches. You don't need a partner, network, or consortium to build your business.

Two pitfalls also loom bright and clear: (1) most small businesses don't have much cash, so at times you must wait for payment on your invoice; and (2) even though the "Big Six" charge $100 an hour or more, small consulting firms can't command that much—$75 is fairly standard in most parts of the country. In spite of these drawbacks, the small business market niche continues to grow. Demand for qualified consulting services is escalating. And as small businesses become mid-size companies opportunities arise to build hourly rates and expand services.

The small businesses referred to in this chapter range from a one-person insurance agency to a manufacturing company with annual sales of $2 million or less. Prospective clients may be in service industries, distribution, manufacturing, or retailing. From a consulting perspective small businesses can be grouped into three categories: start-ups, second-stage companies in operation for two to five years, and mature companies.

It's hard to find even one area in which small businesses do not need help. Most start-ups tend to be undercapitalized and undermanaged. Those companies surviving the start-up phase still search for the best combination of products or services, debt levels, and organization structure. Mature companies often become stagnant and uncreative in solving product/customer problems. They remain undercapitalized, and many continue to have difficulty attracting capable supervisory personnel. Small businesses tend to either expand too rapidly and lose control, or become stagnant and non-competitive. Any way you look at it, they need all the help they can get.

Small business consulting calls for different services at various stages of a client's development. At the start-up stage consulting services generally involve:

- Structuring the company as a corporation, partnership, or proprietorship
- Setting up the business including tax filings, opening bank accounts, and selecting appropriate facilities
- Installing a bookkeeping system
- Originating insurance coverage
- Sourcing start-up capital

During the first two to five years, owners of second-stage companies need help in:

- Developing tax strategies
- Designing and implementing computer based bookkeeping, cost control, and other systems
- Installing cash management controls
- Raising additional capital
- Bank relations
- Business planning
- Compliance reporting

Owners of businesses reaching the mature stage frequently require assistance in:

- Personal financial planning
- Expanding through business acquisitions
- Selling the business

BUSINESS START-UPS

At this stage entrepreneurs generally don't even know what questions to ask. Many believe that all they have to do is borrow money from their friendly banker, rent space, open the doors, put out some advertising, and customers will flock in. When none of these moves works, they wonder why.

Bankers, tax advisors, attorneys, and occasionally SBA personnel offer advice along the way. By the time entrepreneurs recognize the ineffectiveness of this advice they have already borrowed from a bank, incurred substantial unnecessary expenses, and perhaps are already in trouble with the IRS. Now they turn to consultants for a quick fix. Of course, if you can get in the door prior to this free advice, so much the better.

If the client hasn't already incorporated this is a good place to begin. I have helped more than thirty small business clients incorporate through The Company Corporation in Wilmington, Delaware, and have never had a complaint. The cost runs between $150 and $170 and the process takes about ten days. No attorneys are necessary.

Once incorporated, the company must file for a federal identification number and the S election. A set of accounting records must be set up. Bank accounts opened or changed to a more favorable bank. Perhaps leases for office, warehouse, or production space must be negotiated. A business insurance program should be started.

Most beginning entrepreneurs do not have the faintest idea how to arrange any of these opening steps. Consultants not only offer recommendations about what should be done but they also actually perform the activities for the client.

Consulting to business start-ups is a hands-on service. New business owners get so bogged down trying to solicit customers and to get the operation up and running that they seldom have the time or the inclination to get involved in administrative details. This is easy work. None of these steps takes much time. All are essential to get the business moving along. And at this stage, entrepreneurs are generally happy to get the help, even if it does cost a few dollars.

Aside from the pure administrative tasks, consultants can perform an important service for clients by setting up a simple bookkeeping system that conforms to IRS standards. Even if business owners have an accounting background, which most do not, they don't have the time or interest in an activity as mundane as bookkeeping. Simple, inexpensive computer software is readily available (see Chapter 3). Inexpensive software for the preparation of small payrolls and quarterly payroll tax returns can also be purchased.

The most important service you can render start-up clients is to help arrange financing. Rarely do beginning entrepreneurs have any experience borrowing money, other than installment loans for the purchase of cars or a mortgage to buy a home. They usually head directly to the bank holding their personal checking and savings accounts. More often than not they get talked into a second mortgage on their home to collateralize a working capital loan, which invariably leads to problems later on.

Whether refinancing or obtaining initial capital, consultants specializing in the small business niche should be capable of leading clients to the best source of funds and assist in negotiating the best terms. This is all it usually takes to prove your value and generate additional work.

Small Business Administration (SBA)

The local SBA office is a good starting point. Either an SBA-guaranteed bank loan or a direct loan from the agency is the fastest and easiest way to raise start-up capital.

The SBA guarantees, and in some cases lends directly, up to $750,000 for short-term working capital and up to $1 million for equipment and facilities expansion. Although specific SBA criteria change from time to time, the following general rules have remained for several years:

1. A manufacturing company must have under 1,500 employees.
2. A service business must have fewer than $14.5 million in sales.
3. A retailer must have sales under $13.5 million.
4. Transportation and warehousing companies must have fewer than 1,000 employees.
5. Wholesalers must have less than 500 employees.
6. A construction company must have under $9.5 million in sales.

Obviously, a start-up business fits the mold, as do nearly all small businesses in any growth stage. These standards are not sacrosanct, however. In certain states the size range varies, and from time to time the SBA changes its guidelines.

In addition to meeting size criteria, your client must show creditworthiness and meet five general credit standards. The business owner must:

1. Prove personal integrity and good character.
2. Show evidence of ability to operate the business successfully.
3. Have enough personal capital in the business to demonstrate that with SBA assistance the business will be operated on a sound financial basis. The implication that a financially sound debt/equity ratio is required to get SBA help seems absurd, but that's what the SBA wants.

4. Must be "of such sound value or so secured as reasonably to assure repayment," to quote the original Small Business Act.

5. Must show that the company's historical financial performance and projected performance after receiving the loan warrant repayment out of future earnings. Obviously, only projected performance relates to start-up businesses.

SBA Bank Loan Guarantees

Applicants for SBA assistance must first be turned down by at least two commercial lenders. If the SBA chooses to participate, it will guarantee 90 percent of a loan up to $155,000 and 85 percent of the balance, up to $1 million. Participating banks must carry the remainder. Many banks refuse to consider participation with the SBA, however, because of stringent rules, interest rate limits, and lengthy terms. Interest rates for SBA guaranteed loans range from 2.25 to 2.75 over prime. Terms run up to 25 years.

SBA Direct Loans

Failing to get an SBA-guaranteed loan, your client might try for a direct loan, although these are hard to arrange. The SBA's willingness to go this route depends on how much they have left from the current year allocation from Congress, which is usually zero.

SBA guarantees and direct loans have special provisions for minorities: business owners that fit the SBA's definition get preferential treatment. Any type of business qualifies for SBA assistance except publishing, gambling, and investment or speculation in real estate.

Business and Industrial Development Company

One recent variation in the normal SBA program is the sale of SBA guaranteed loans on the open market, which takes the bank and the SBA out entirely. The Business and Industrial Development Company (BIDCO), a private organization originated in California, supports the open market in that state. A few other states have followed suit and expanded the concept to include equity funding as well as debt.

Special SBA Programs The SBA also supports special programs to meet specific needs, either with direct loans or guarantees. Here are the major ones:

1. Economic Opportunity Loans for economic or socially disadvantaged entrepreneurs. Blacks, hispanics, American Indians, and native Alaskans are examples of those defined as disadvantaged.

2. Disaster Loans for businesses in federally declared disaster areas resulting from floods, earthquakes, tornadoes, and so on.

3. Handicapped Assistance Loans for either physically handicapped business owners or those companies where more than 75 percent of the employees are handicapped in some fashion.

4. Economic Injury Loans for businesses injured by some government action, such as the closing of military installations, federal acts involving pollution or safety requirements, and so on.

5. Displaced Business Loans for companies displaced by a government act such as building a road through the middle of the client's facility.

6. Contract Loan Program for businesses that have been in operation more than twelve months on specific government contracts to enable them to complete the contract. This only covers labor and materials.

7. Seasonal Line of Credit for seasonal businesses.

8. Contractor and Real Estate Loans of up to three years for the construction of commercial or residential properties.

If your client fits one of these definitions you should be able to raise capital without much difficulty.

SBA Surety Bond Guaranty Program

This program provides guarantees for small building contractors who cannot afford the exorbitant charges for a surety bond. The SBA guarantees up to 90 percent of the losses incurred by a surety company granting the bond. This usually reduces the premium to a manageable level. Construction contracts cannot exceed $100,000 for the 90 percent guarantee and $1,250,000 for an 80 percent guarantee.

If the SBA doesn't work out, the Economic Development Agency is another interesting possibility, assuming your client is in the right business and the right location.

The Economic Development Agency (EDA)

The Economic Development Agency provides business development loans to construct or upgrade a specific community, neighborhood, or area. The money must be used to develop a business that creates new jobs and improves the income level and conditions for local residents. The new or expanding business must be in an EDA-designated redevelopment area. EDA loans do not have an upper limit. Projects already carrying SBA guarantees get preferential treatment because then the EDA merely increases the amount of the bank guarantee.

Direct EDA loans are made for up to 80 percent of the purchase price of hard assets. Interest rates range from prime plus 1.5 percent to 2.5 percent with the term limited to the life of the asset up to twenty-five years. In addition to the interest rate, the EDA charges an annual placement, or guarantee, fee of one-half percent of the outstanding balance of the loan. Working capital loans are also available with the EDA guaranteeing 90 percent for a term of five years.

In addition to being located in a redevelopment area, the project must meet seven criteria:

1. The project must be consistent with the EDA's Overall Economic Development Program (OEDP).
2. Each applicant must first get the approval of the state or municipal agency promoting the development.
3. The business cannot be in an industry experiencing significant overcapacity.
4. The business must justify its ability to repay the loan.
5. The applicant must provide at least 15 percent equity in the project.
6. Any construction contractors on the project must pay prevailing government pay scales.
7. Only those projects which provide an EDA exposure of $20,000 or less per job created, or saved, will be considered.

EDA financing clearly isn't for everyone, but it's an interesting possibility if the shoe fits.

Marketing

Start-up businesses are probably the easiest and most straightforward to market of any category of prospective clients. Nearly every approach described in Chapter 4 works. A combination of the following generally brings excellent results quickly:

1. Direct mail. Every week, city newspapers list new business start-ups, complete with company name and address. Public accountants, usually the first stop for a new business owner, are another good target for a mail campaign.

2. Local SBA office. Registering with the SBA gets you on the list of recommended consultants. Participation in a local SCORE chapter helps at times, but usually causes more problems than it solves. Presentations at small business start-up seminars work well.

3. Advertising. Local newspapers, television channels, radio talk shows are all effective.

4. Referrals. Local banks and small law firms are especially helpful.

5. Public relations. Participation in local chamber of commerce, civic clubs, golf, tennis and health clubs puts you in the limelight.

6. Municipal and industry local trade groups. Attendance at meetings, seminars, and conferences provides an audience for business card distribution.

These tactics all work reasonably well. Some are more effective than others, depending upon where you are located and how many clients you want to attract.

Organization and Fees

Start-up engagements are relatively short-lived. They don't require long absences from the office. Requirements for special training or technical knowledge are minimal. Consequently, sole practitioners find this niche easy to manage both for production and marketing. The market is characterized by a large number of clients and short engagements.

If you can get clients before they open their doors, fees run slightly higher than after the business is up and running. The longer an entrepreneur is in business before calling you, the less equity money remains for your fees. However, once you get the client a bank loan consulting fees become more palatable.

Start-up engagements should never be billed at an hourly rate. Too often, the amount of non-productive time explaining the rules of the game adds up to more than clients can afford. Much better to charge flat fees for the engagement and make up the difference in additional assignments as the business grows.

SECOND STAGE BUSINESSES

Once a business has been in operation for two or three years it has reached the second stage of development. Now an entirely new series of problems confront the owner, providing consultants with even greater opportunities.

Businesses in this stage have breached the first barricades to producing and selling their products or services. They have met debt service obligations for a few years. They have acquired facilities and production equipment. They probably have a payroll of two to ten people. They are in the process of developing a market reputation. By now they should be turning a profit and positive cash flow. Perhaps a public accountant prepares quarterly payroll returns and even performs monthly bookkeeping services. Companies have progressed from the first stage of development to the second stage.

A second set of hurdles now includes worrying about tax strategies, improving operating systems, cash management, and complying with municipal, state, and federal regulations. Also by this time, owners begin thinking about planning for the future, and this means preparing a business plan. To achieve future growth, the company will most likely need additional capital, either equity or long-term debt. Consultants with resources at their fingertips can provide significant assistance in overcoming all of these second stage hurdles.

In most cases the client's public accountant provides adequate tax advice. More often than not, however, without a detailed knowledge of the business and the owner's strategic plans, public accountants can only give advice about short-term tax savings tactics. Given a working knowledge of federal and state tax laws, consultants should be in a position to integrate short-term tactics with long-term tax strategies which maximize income to the business owners. Long-range strategies might encompass a business investment program, multiple corporations, family income splitting, off-shore entities, and a number of other options that an external tax advisor can't see.

Consultants can also help design and implement cost control and cash management systems. Perhaps they can arrange for a service bureau to prepare payrolls and payroll tax returns, or change to a bank lockbox system to hasten collections. Maybe a budgetary control system makes sense, or an integrated production and inventory control system. At this stage, operating systems are significantly easier to design and install than those described in Chapter 5 for more developed companies.

For clients needing second stage financing, the first step is to prepare a business plan. Small business owners seldom have the time or the experience to do this job effectively and usually bring in consultants to prepare the business plan and source the capital.

The preparation of business plans necessitates at least a cursory attempt at strategic planning. Business owners usually hate to spend time on such an esoteric exercise and you frequently end up doing the entire job, with client approval of course. Once a business plan has been completed, you can convert it into a financing plan and begin sourcing funds.

As described previously, the SBA and the EDA both provide financing assistance during second stage expansion as well as for initial start-up capital. Other potential sources are:

1. Larger regional banks. Now that the entrepreneur has proven business credentials and the company has some hard assets, larger banks give a much warmer reception to requests for term loans.

2. Small Business Investment Companies (SBICs). Many regional banks have SBIC divisions. These pseudo-venture capital operations are a good source for both term loans and small amounts of equity capital. They seldom demand more than a 15 percent ownership interest. A financing package can usually marry SBIC participation with parent-bank term loans.

3. Private venture capital firms and small investment banks. These financing houses look for high average annual returns on their investment (frequently exceeding 30 percent) and a significant investment appreciation over a five-year period. Many expect the client to go public in four to five years.

4. Leasing. Clients rarely think of leasing as a means of financing expansion, mainly because they don't know where to find appropriate leasing companies or how to negotiate the best terms. Consultants can play a major role in both activities.

In addition to financing, systems, and tax planning, consultants who service second stage clients need a good grasp of compliance reporting requirements from municipal, state, and federal agencies. Clients frequently get into trouble because they do not file the appropriate reports on time, or else they ignore them completely. Many business owners don't have the vaguest idea when each of the myriad of reports is required.

Marketing

Some of the same marketing tactics employed for getting start-up clients apply to second stage companies, with one major difference in approach. Owners of second stage companies are usually so bogged down in daily business problems that they seldom have time to attend conferences, meetings, or seminars. They get caught between the need for outside assistance and the lack of time to locate qualified consultants. Marketing efforts, therefore, must be structured to bring your name to the attention of business owners at their place of business.

Direct mailings consisting of tax tips, financing ideas, small business software recommendations, and creative marketing thoughts have proven effective tactics for penetrating this market.

Several years ago, I devised a one-page flyer that I mailed bimonthly to prospective clients in my county. Each flyer concentrated on one set of creative operating ideas. One provided tips on long-range tax planning, another included ideas for revamping an insurance package, a third highlighted new financing methods, and so on. The response was remarkable. Over a twelve-month period I picked up seventeen new clients, some for short-term projects, several for longer-term engagements.

Another good marketing tactic calls for continued alliances with local public accounting firms. Small business owners rely on their outside accountants for tax, banking, and, to some extent, systems advice. Although some such firms actively solicit consulting work, many more would rather concentrate on their specialties and refer such work to full-time consultants.

Some small law firms can also be helpful, although most lawyers seem to be non-business oriented and not interested in providing consulting leads. Opportunities for referrals from banks vary, depending on the bank's current portfolio, its size, and the business acumen of bank managers. Few consultants get much help from SBA contacts at this stage, unless a company has defaulted on an SBA loan.

Organization and Fees

Although second stage engagements exhibit many of the characteristics of start-up work, some variations also exist. Jobs are more complex, requiring a stronger background in general management and more technical capabilities. Many become extended engagements lasting six to nine months. Some require limited travel. A good portion of the work can be performed at the client's site, however, or in your office.

Most sole practitioners can continue servicing second stage clients indefinitely without partnership help. Occasionally, consortium consultants can be called in to help with extended engagements or technical specialties. Networking with small public accounting firms and sole practitioner lawyers brings additional talent to your pool.

As the number of clients grows it's helpful to structure a formal office with at least one person available to cover the telephone and type reports. Many consulting firms get by with part-time help for several years, however.

Fees are normally billed at hourly rates. As with all small business clients, rates tend to be less than those billed to larger clients. They typically range from $75 to $100 an hour. On the plus side, however, because of the potentially large base of clients, nearly continuous work loads, and little need for large amounts of marketing time, annual billable hours are much higher than in other niche markets. Monthly retainers could be used for certain jobs, although most small clients prefer to pay after the fact. If the client isn't in financial difficulty, retainers should not be required.

MATURE BUSINESSES

Small companies that have matured over a period of years, require significantly different types of consulting services. They still need tax, systems, and financing help, and perhaps some long-range planning or recruiting assistance, but these are corollary to a business owner's major concerns at this stage. Owners now begin to look at ways to maximize the personal benefits they can derive from the company. Assuming the company is still profitable, they also begin looking at possible expansion moves. Consultants play a major role in both areas.

Personal Financial Planning

Personal financial planning for business owners is such a hot market that it's surprising how many capable management consultants have abdicated this work to public accountants and financial planners. Consultants are in a much better position to advise business owners than either of these professionals simply because they understand the intricacies of the client's business. They approach personal planning from the perspective of maximizing personal benefits from business cash, rather than from after-tax take home pay.

Public accountants stress tax savings. Financial planners emphasize life insurance and personal investments. While tax savings, life insurance, and personal investing are important adjuncts of personal financial planning, without being integrated with the many personal gains to be derived from the business they fall short of a complete plan.

Consultants can help business owners devise a personal financial plan to accomplish three objectives:

1. Maximize the use of tax-free or pre-tax business cash for personal benefits.

2. Structure a business investment program that maximizes retirement income.

3. Develop a strategy for building estate assets.

A corollary program to protect personal and business assets should also be implemented.

Business Cash for Personal Use

The essence of maximizing the personal use of business cash revolves around tactical tax planning. You don't have to be a tax expert, but knowing the main small business tax gimmicks is essential. With a rudimentary background in preparing tax returns, even if only your own, it shouldn't take long to brush up.

Helpful tax books abound. The annual edition of the CCH U.S. Master Tax Guide is a good start. Some of the best tax savings techniques are: S corporation income splitting, independent contractor employees, intercompany loans, definitions and treatment of business expenses, and the utilization of family employees. The main idea is to structure the business in such a way that the owner can withdraw cash or use business cash to pay personal expenses while minimizing taxes.

Maximizing Retirement Income

Retirement planning is more complex. Although identifying the various forms of life insurance is a simplistic approach and only a partial solution to the real dilemma, it is a good beginning. The major objective should be to fund retirement programs with the company's pre-tax dollars and then to ensure that the stream of income will be available for retirement.

In addition to life insurance, several tactics serve the purpose: the use of multiple corporations and partnerships, company-funded retirement plans, long-term investment programs using company cash, various types of trusts, and off-shore investing. My book *Tap The Hidden Wealth in Your Business* (McGraw-Hill) explains each of these tactics in depth. Another helpful reference is, *The Financial Planner's Guide to Estate Planning* by Paul J. Lochray (Prentice-Hall).

Maximizing Estate Assets

In most cases, the business itself represents an owner's largest and most valuable asset. Maximizing estate assets involves not only thorough planning for retirement income; it also encompasses a plan to safeguard the owner's business interest and then convert this interest into cash at the appropriate time.

Structuring an asset protection plan for business owners is one of the most welcome services you can perform. While protecting a homestead, bank accounts, and personal investments is certainly an important step, protecting an owner's interest in the business is crucial. Nefarious lawyers convince too many courts to award judgments that wipe out small businesses, leaving nothing for retirement years or for an estate. Careful structuring with trusts, family members, and multiple corporations can prevent this from happening.

Maximizing estate assets also consists of converting an owner's business interest into cash by selling it either to a chosen successor or on the open market. Family members, employees, partners, even customers and suppliers make viable successor candidates. You should be in an ideal position to help the owner develop a plan for bringing one of these successors into the business and structuring a buyout agreement well in advance of retirement.

If successor ownership does not appear feasible, you could help the owner develop a strategic plan to sell the company on the open market. Getting maximum value for a small business can be a complex undertaking and may require several years to achieve. Consultants are in a position to help business owners achieve this goal by offering assistance in several areas: valuing the company, cleaning up contingencies and otherwise getting it ready for sale, sourcing buyers, assisting buyers to arrange financing, negotiating the terms and conditions of sales, and finally coordinating the preparation of the buy/sell agreement.

Future Expansion

Small business owners have a propensity for dreaming about expanding the company into a major force in the market without ever taking actions to make it happen. They don't fulfill these dreams because they seldom have either the time or the knowledge to put together a meaningful growth plan or to implement it once prepared. Small businesses are not complex. It doesn't take very long to lend a hand for planning and implementing such moves.

Expansion plans might involve an additional facility, new product introductions, a change in markets, an export program, or the acquisition of a going business. Given the right circumstances the latter frequently fulfills the owner's desire for expansion while simultaneously increasing cash flow. With a little prodding from a trusted consultant, owners frequently take this route as the fastest and most lucrative way to expand.

Once the owner decides to make an acquisition you should be able to carry the ball through the entire process. Acquisitions of small businesses differ from the type of M & A work described in Chapter 5. In most cases the deals are small with target candidates located in the immediate vicinity. Financing usually combines a note from your client and a small bank loan. Small business acquisitions move along very rapidly, seldom taking more than three or four months.

The biggest problem usually results from a lack of management in the company being acquired. When your client is suddenly faced with the need to manage two companies instead of one, you can help by proposing systems, cash management techniques, and control measures to make the task less painful.

Marketing

One of the real benefits in the small business market niche is the evolutionary nature of clients. Very often personal financial planning and expansion assistance come naturally as the client matures. Initial engagements may be short-lived, but repeat business is almost a foregone conclusion. Once you do a satisfactory job in the early stages, clients seldom switch to someone else as the company grows.

Referrals usually work best for getting new clients at the mature stage. As with second stage clients, public accountants, lawyers, and bankers are all helpful. In addition, small business owners usually belong to one or more local civic groups—Lions, Rotary, Kiwanis, chamber of commerce, and so on. Active participation gets you valuable introductions. A presentation now and then helps authenticate your credentials as a small business consultant. Export trade groups, tax conferences, and personal financial or estate planning seminars also help. Occasionally, consultants find that teaching adult education courses gives them an entry competitors miss.

Organization and Fees

The more engagements you take with mature stage clients the more essential it becomes to work with a network of other specialists. Although many jobs are relatively simple and can be managed quite well by a sole practitioner, special expertise in tax, legal matters, estate planning, and other topics is frequently called for. Whereas multi-partner firms generally have all the required expertise within the firm, networking enables sole practitioners and small partnerships to compete effectively.

Fees are handled in the same manner as for second stage jobs. Hourly rates without retainers continue to be the most common. Mature stage clients, however, generally have more cash to work with and, therefore, higher rates can be charged, typically between $80 and $120 an hour.

HAZARDS AND SOLUTIONS

Small business clients are notorious for expecting consultants to be babysitters. As we all know, clients large or small want us to be on call twenty-four hours a day, seven days a week to answer questions and perform services far beyond the original scope of the engagement. Small business owners go one step further. The questions asked are often inane and simplistic, questions that anyone running a business should be able to answer, or at least be able to get answered from their accounting and legal professionals. For example, a good friend specializing in small accounts, was a former practicing CPA and had a wealth of experience preparing business and personal tax returns. He was also very conscientious.

Although this ex-CPA sold his tax practice years earlier and had intentionally stayed away from engagements involving any type of tax work, clients continued to bombard him with tax questions: How should I depreciate my computer equipment? What are the new rules about business use of personal cars? Can I take my 21 year-old daughter as a dependent? How do I set up an IRA? One year my friend took a vacation to the Virgin Islands and mistakenly left the phone number of his resort with clients. The phone never stopped ringing. He finally gave up. To the chagrin of his family, they checked out early and returned home. He has yet to solve the babysitting problem.

Business babysitting is an occupational hazard of small business consulting. There doesn't seem to be any ready solution. If you want to be in this business you might as well structure your time and your firm to handle such extraneous requests. The trick is to turn non-billable hours answering inane questions into billable hours and extended engagements, without aggravating the client.

There aren't any fool-proof ways to avoid the issue completely, but the following procedures do reduce pesky client calls and at the same time generally promote increased business.

1. Scope agreement. As far as possible outline your understanding of the specific projects a client wants performed. Most clients won't adhere to it once you get involved, but at least it serves as a referral document for later disputes.

2. Monthly retainer. If it appears that the engagement will entail more general counseling than project work, set up a monthly retainer. This allows you to dedicate a fixed number of hours per month to that client. Make it clear right from the start that this is all the time you have available. Clients generally respect your obligation to service other accounts.

3. Allocate days. For continuous counseling work, allocate certain days of the week or month to the client. Let the owner know that these are the only days you will be available for consultation. This works reasonably well in conjunction with monthly retainers.

4. Segregate hourly rates. Establish hourly billing rates that vary with the type of work performed: the highest rate attributable to the work most valued by your client. For example, based on an average rate of $100 per hour, charge $35 for filing payroll tax returns, $50 for general bookkeeping and compliance reports, $75 for systems and personnel recruiting projects, $100 for arranging financing, $125 for tax advice, and $150 for personal financial counseling. Or alternately, charge the higher rates for those areas causing the most aggravation. Flat fees for selling a business or making an acquisition can more than make up for time wasted on other work.

5. *Refer work.* Regardless of attempts to limit babysitting calls, some clients persist. A number of these calls can probably be handled more efficiently by specialists. I usually refer clients with tax questions to CPAs, those with legal questions to lawyers, personal investing questions to financial planners or stock brokers, and so on. Not only does the client probably get better advice, but by referring clients to other professionals, you almost always get referrals back.

No tactic works equally well with all clients. Business babysitting remains a permanent fixture in this market niche. These ideas mitigate the problem but do not cure. Most consultants who have been in the small business market for some time caution newcomers to stay away if they can't put up with at least some amount of extraneous questions and non-billable hours.

On the plus side, small business consulting is growing rapidly. The market assures continuous clients and a wide variety of work. Most engagements stimulate your imagination by requiring creative answers. And the rewards go beyond monetary gain. It's hard to beat the personal satisfaction of husbanding a small business through its start-up and growth stages and then see it blossom into a viable, profitable entity.

For the mercenary minded, more than one high fee engagement has evolved from sticking with a small business until it became large enough to warrant sophisticated consulting.

11 Government Contracting Market

The federal government remains the largest customer for nearly every product in practically every industry. As it continues to enjoy super-power status, increasing its personnel, and multiplying its give-away programs, the government will inevitably continue to demand more and more products and services and more technologically advanced solutions to its problems. The government does, and will continue to, purchase shoe laces, bakery goods, consulting services, tanks, bullets, computer software, aspirins, application engineering, classroom instruction, and literally millions of other types of products and services from companies of every size and shape.

The mix of government needs shifts from time to time but the amount of money paid out to suppliers is increasing geometrically. Prime contracts placed by the federal government with just the top twenty-five contractors ran in excess of $90 billion in 1990. Total outstanding federal contracts exceed $250 billion even with budget cutbacks.

Prime contractors such as Boeing, IBM, General Electric, and Dupont are not the only beneficiaries. Beneath these prime contractors resides layer upon layer of smaller sub-contractors. Literally hundreds of thousands of companies and millions of employees depend on federal procurement for a livelihood. More than 90 percent of awarded contracts are for less than $25,000 and placed with small businesses!

Every year new smaller and mid-size companies enter this burgeoning market. Many remain ill-equipped to cope with the myriad of bidding and performance regulations. Many more would attempt entry if they knew how to get on a bidders' list. Still more would try their hand if they understood how to comply with the complex, unique rules of this modified version of a market economy.

Two vastly different consulting markets exist in government contract work. The first relates to producers of goods and services who utilize consulting expertise to source, bid, negotiate, and comply with government contracts. The second focuses on selling consulting services direct to the federal government.

Although the latter remains an important growth market, its breadth and complexity are so great that entire books have been written on the subject. Many consulting jobs require engineering, design, or construction backgrounds. The machinations required to bid jobs, the stringent regulations to be followed in performing the work, and the political influence necessary to be successful in the field make the subject far too encompassing for one chapter in a book of this scope.

Consequently, the remainder of this chapter focuses on the former market, providing consulting services to smaller and mid-size companies either already involved in government contracting as prime or sub-contractors or wishing to enter the market.

Several federal programs favor small business contractors by intentionally setting aside funds for specific categories of companies. Some of the more popular set-aside procurements are for:

- Any small business meeting the Small Business Administration (SBA) definition by Standard Industrial Classification (SIC) code

- Socially disadvantaged small businesses at least 51 percent owned and managed by individuals subject to racial, ethnic, religious, or cultural bias

- Economically disadvantaged small businesses at least 51 percent owned by socially disadvantaged individuals unable to obtain capital or credit in the free market

- Small businesses at least 51 percent owned by women

- Businesses owned 100 percent by minorities
- Economically and socially disadvantaged businesses at least 51 percent owned and operated by minority groups
- Business located in high unemployment areas of the country

In addition to preferential treatment given to companies falling within these categories, federal law requires prime contractors to sub-contract work to small businesses. To promote competition in the bidding process, the government has established an office of "Competition Advocate" to ensure full and open competition in all federal procurement.

The Small Business Innovation Research (SBIR) program sets aside a percentage of the annual budgets of all major federal departments and agencies for contract grants to small businesses involved in research projects. Small construction firms benefit by a 10 percent set aside goal for projects involving embassy buildings. Minority owned businesses get an additional 10 percent of the projects for these properties.

Plenty of opportunities exist for smaller companies in government contracting, and that translates into enormous opportunities for consulting engagements. As with all government work, the complexity of the bid process and performance regulations keep many otherwise qualified competitors out of the market. In addition to attracting many new clients eager to enter government contracting markets, consulting specialists can expand existing client work by encouraging them to sell to the government. Between the two, you should find more than enough business to keep you busy for years to come.

OPPORTUNITIES

Clients selling to the federal government need consulting help in nine areas:

1. Matching the company's product line with federal procurement needs
2. Getting on the appropriate bid list

3. Preparing and submitting the bid package
4. Negotiating bid terms with procurement agencies
5. Filing progress payment requests
6. Complying with contract quality standards
7. Implementing appropriate cost accounting systems
8. Coordinating government audits
9. Submitting post-contract claims

Not all clients need assistance in all areas. Some already have efficient cost accounting systems. Others have little difficulty complying with quality standards. Many can handle their own negotiations. Frequently consultants are engaged to manage specific portions of the bid process, such as writing the bid package, or coordinating government audits. Clients that are new to government work generally need assistance in all areas, at least their first time through the process.

Companies that successfully complete one contract usually have opportunities for follow-on work. The range of assistance may shift for the second or third contract, but, generally, once you get in the door, clients welcome additional help for follow-on work. This assures you of a continual flow of repeat business.

Matching a Client's Products with Procurement Needs

The fastest way to locate the appropriate government agency that purchases specific products or services is to request a copy of the latest procurement bidding list from a local procurement office. If your client's products are military oriented, contact the navy, air force, or army procurement office. If they relate to environmental protection call the EPA; if public health oriented call the National Health Service, and so on.

If a client's products do not readily relate to a specific agency, pick up a copy of the *U.S. Government Purchasing and Sales Directory*. Most SBA offices can order one for you if they don't have it in stock. This directory is probably the best common source for determining the type of products each agency buys. It includes:

- A listing of products and services purchased by three federal supply groups: major civilian purchasing offices, major military procurement agencies, and local military installations that do their own procurement
- A cross reference of the names and addresses of specific procurement agencies
- A designation of federal agencies funding research and development projects
- A guide to government specifications

The directory also includes copies of government forms, information about federal property sales, and supplemental information for preparing proposals.

Another good source of upcoming contract bids is the *Commerce Business Daily*. This publication lists all the requests for proposals (called RFPs) for everything the government buys. It is the "want ad" newspaper for government procurements and the prime source of information about services (as opposed to product) needs. Consultants can use its listing of awards to prime contractors as leads for soliciting sub-contract work.

Once a client determines which agency to sell to, it must get on that agency's bidders' list. Consultants can be extremely helpful in assisting the client complete a Standard Form SF 129 to accomplish this. You should also register your client with the interagency Procurement Automated Source System (PASS) which provides lists of qualified bidders to prime contractors and agencies when the original bid process doesn't bring sufficient results.

Getting on a bidders' list is a good first step. But to land a government contract the next rung must be climbed, and that entails constant follow-up with the relevant procurement agency. Consultants can handle this chore much more effectively than clients and should play a major role in extracting bid solicitations.

Before preparing a bid package the client must have two operating systems in place that meet government standards: a quality control system, and a cost accounting system. Consultants should be in an excellent position to assist clients design and install new systems or revamp and upgrade existing systems.

Quality Control Systems

Although each government contract may require special features to ensure specified product quality levels, federal standards mandate seven elements in all quality control systems.

1. Responsibility. A single individual must be responsible for the quality control organization. Subordinates may be responsible for each of the quality assurance steps in the process, but the quality control manager handles any interface with government quality auditors.

2. Quality planning. The manufacturing process must be so designed as to build in quality at each step. Methods for ensuring this are detailed in a quality assurance procedure manual that must be continuously updated by the quality control manager.

3. Specification control. Every individual in the production cycle must have ready access to the technical product specifications as well as the procedures for inspecting, testing, and shipping products.

4. Material control. Procedures must be implemented to ensure that materials/components received from suppliers meet contract specifications.

5. Measurement and test equipment control. The company must maintain sufficient measurement and test equipment to ensure specification compliance. These tools must be regularly calibrated and stored in a secure environment.

6. Defective material control. Defective raw material or in-process parts must be identified, segregated, and either reworked to specification or destroyed to be certain that they do not get shipped to the customer.

7. Record keeping and reports. A formal record keeping system must be in place to record each step in the production, inspecting, testing, and shipping process. Reports of deficiencies must be regularly filed.

In addition, quality systems for products manufactured to life support specifications must maintain records of each material and component in the product all the way back to its origin. In the case of steel parts, for example, the material must be traceable back to the original mill run. This tracking ability is called "traceability."

Clients manufacturing products to critical military specifications may have to get their products pre-qualified as to quality and performance before becoming registered as a qualified bidder. Client egos tend to get in the way of meeting this requirement. Consultants, on the other hand, can walk the product through the pre-qualification stage with appropriate procurement officials as part of the selection and bidding process without getting client personnel involved.

The SBA puts out an excellent pamphlet describing the type of quality control system contractors should implement. It is entitled "Setting Up a Quality Control System, MA-243, Management Aids for Small Manufacturers" and can be obtained from local SBA offices or directly from the SBA's Washington headquarters. Another valuable source of information is the "Guide to Quality Control Systems and Written Procedures" put out by the General Services Administration. It can be obtained from the GSA, ROB, Room 1050, 7th and D Streets, Washington, DC 20407, (202) 708-5804.

Cost Accounting System

Most manufacturing companies maintain some semblance of a cost accounting system but probably have not seen the necessity of bringing it up to government standards. This presents an excellent opportunity for separate project work. If a client has any inclination to enter government contracting, a functional cost accounting system is mandatory. For larger contracts, and for all military specification work, the system must meet the Cost Accounting Standards Board criteria.

The advent of quick computer-generated information has blurred the commercial necessity for accurate cost accumulation by specific product. Many manufacturing companies, especially smaller ones, have relegated cost accounting to the back burner as an antiquated discipline. The government doesn't agree. In fact, all prices in government bids are based on the cost to make the product plus a profit markup, normally 10 to 15 percent over actual cost.

The larger the government contract the more important accurate cost accounting systems must be. If a company expects to land a contract in excess of $25,000 it must have a qualified cost accounting system in place and functioning. What better way to achieve this than with a consultant's expertise?

Within the bid package, the foundation of the bid price rests on the company's estimate of the actual costs to produce the products. For larger bids, these estimates must show the detailed build-up of material, labor, direct overhead, and allocated overhead costs per unit.

For new bidders as well as for others about whom the procurement agency does not feel it has enough information to evaluate a bid, a preaward survey is a very real possibility. It is conducted by the Defense Contract Administration Services (DCAS), the agency responsible for administering contracts. Two of the most critical areas surveyed are the quality control system and the cost accounting system. Preaward surveys are routinely performed when:

- The contract exceeds $25,000.
- The company has not previously done business with the government.
- The product or service is deemed critical to life support.
- The government is significantly increasing its business with the contractor.
- The company has had problems with previous contracts.

The presence of a consultant during this survey greatly enhances the chances of a client getting the contract award. DCAS auditors prefer to have someone around who can answer questions quickly and accurately and who does not have a proprietary interest in the contract award. Such independent appraisals of operating systems and personnel frequently tilt the results of a preaward survey in favor of the client.

At a later date, after the contract has been awarded and the client delivers products, Defense Contracts Audit Administration (DCAA) auditors will return to verify the actual costs by unit accumulated against the original estimate. DCAS auditors will also return to verify compliance with quality and other engineering standards. In both cases, consulting assistance can be invaluable.

Someone must husband the government auditors through the company's cost accounting system. If you have been instrumental in designing and implementing the system in the first place, it's doubtful that client personnel could move the auditor through as fast. And speed is of the essence. The faster you can get DCAA and DCAS people through the audit the less likelihood of serious deficiency adjustments. The timing and frequency of government audits depends on several factors: size of the contract, type of materiel purchased, number of sources of the same product, and the government agency doing the buying. In some cases—notably for major military contracts—government auditors might maintain full time residency at the company's facility. For less critical products, or those with lower quality standards, audits may be quarterly, annually, or at the end of the contract period.

The Bid Package

Before a bid can be awarded a bid package (proposal) must be submitted. In addition to per-unit prices adding up to the total contract value, the bid package contains a variety of information that enables the procurement officer to judge the company's responsibility and responsiveness. To government procurement officers, responsibility means that a company has:

- Adequate financial resources to complete the contract or has the ability to raise sufficient capital
- A satisfactory performance record on previous contracts
- The capability of meeting required delivery dates in conjunction with complying with its other government and commercial obligations
- Qualified as being otherwise acceptable to making the award under applicable laws and regulations

Responsiveness relates to a company's compliance with the specifications and other requirements contained in the Request For Proposal (RFP). Bids can, at the discretion of the procurement officer, be disqualified as nonresponsive if:

- An authorized company official has not signed it.
- The delivery schedule is not stated in compliance with the solicitation.

- The bid is made conditional upon receiving other contracts or other segments of the same contract.
- A fixed unit price and total contract price have not been stated.
- Any exceptions are taken to the solicitation clauses.

Consultants can't do much about helping a client prove it is a responsible contractor but they can play a major role in making sure the bid package is responsive. Much of the package resembles a standard financing plan submitted for commercial loans. Some sections require greater detail.

The size of a bid package varies with the type of product being proposed and the amount of the contract. It can range from ten or twelve pages of forms and brief descriptions to several volumes each several inches thick. The following, however, are common elements for inclusion in nearly all bid packages:

1. Cost build-up to contract price
2. Description of company
3. Qualifications of management and technical expertise
4. Description of quality control system
5. Description of accounting/cost system
6. Description of facilities

The RFP includes appropriate formats to display estimated cost build-ups. If these are not adequate the client can construct its own calculations, as long as adequate descriptive material is also included.

The history, business, and ownership structure of the company should be described in sufficient detail to give the reader a clear indication that the company is qualified to do the job. It should emphasize the stability, reputation, and general market acceptance of the company's products or services. As with other customers, the government doesn't want to do business with a company on the brink of failure or that has a poor industry reputation.

If the bid falls under the small business allocation regulations or other special award criteria, care must be taken to clearly identify why the company qualifies for the exception. Too often, even consultants forget to lay out these facts and a bid is lost because the procurement officer doesn't recognize the bidder's qualifications.

A description of management qualification and technical expertise must always be included. Proof of a company's ability to do the job is crucial. A company submitting a low bid without demonstrable qualified expertise invariably fails the responsibility test.

In addition to brief profiles of the experience and background of its key management personnel, the company must state which key personnel, if any, are not U.S. citizens. This is critical for military and many other life support contracts. Engineered products require evidence of sufficient technical knowledge to design or produce the product.

The quality control section should specifically state positive answers to the previously described quality criteria.

For larger or more complex contracts a complete description of the cost accounting system should be included. This should clearly identify how and why it meets government cost accounting standards.

RFPs for smaller contracts or less critical products need only include two or three descriptive sentences.

A description of the facilities—both real estate and production capacity—must be included to prove that enough capacity exists to handle the project. If additional equipment or space is needed, proof of a company's ability to acquire such facilities in time to meet delivery requirements must be presented.

Sound consulting advice in the preparation of a bid package can easily make the difference between a successful bid and one that falls flat. Consultants can make sure that clients fully understand what product specifications and other requirements the RFP calls for and can then assist and verify that client personnel have fully complied. All required information must be supplied or the company will be considered nonresponsive. Answers to questions and descriptive material should be specific, not rambling generalities.

The prose sections should be written with clarity, forcefulness, and confidence. Many times consultants can write these sections in much better form than client personnel. Consultants are also in a good position to assist the client research competition sufficiently to make the bid price competitive. If negotiations with procurement officers are necessary you might be called upon to assist client personnel structure negotiating tactics and even participate in the negotiation, if requested.

Postaward Activities

After a contract has been awarded and the client begins producing and delivering products, your role shifts and becomes that of a coordinator. As flocks of government auditors, procurement officers, and inspectors descend on a client's facility, you should be in a position to coordinate the gathering of data and be ready to answer and explain variations from the original RFP.

If the contract involves progress payments, consultants can assist client personnel calculate and submit monthly payment requests. When clients miss deliveries, run into quality problems, or have products rejected for any reason, you should be able to smooth the way with procurement officers. In the government contracting arena, continual diplomacy nets additional follow-on work. Brash responses frequently kill future opportunities. Consultants are usually in a much better position than client personnel to handle procurement interfaces diplomatically. Once you prove yourself in this area, you will more than earn your keep for a long time to come.

CONTINUITY OF ENGAGEMENTS

One of the hallmarks of government contracting consulting is that engagements never seem to end. The scope of these engagements is so broad, and client recognition of the importance of having a qualified consultant in tow is so pervasive, that once you get in the door follow-on engagements seem to flow like a springtime mountain stream.

Not all engagements are the same, however. More project work comes up with clients new-to-government contracting. Cost accounting systems, quality control programs, facilities rearrangement projects, competitive market research, matching client products with government agencies, and so on, all take on added significance. In addition, these clients require more detailed guidance in learning the ropes. In many respects new-to-government contracting clients need more hand-holding than actual consulting work.

Advanced contracting clients rely on your ability to keep procurement officers and auditors honest, satisfied, and at bay. Negotiating with DCAS and DCAA auditors can become a major effort.

Filing claims for extra work, renegotiating contracts, and follow-on procurement efforts are all important projects. Negotiating adjustments in progress payment requests, coordinating progress payments with suppliers, interfacing with procurement organizations, continual research into competitors' capabilities all consume additional billable hours.

Eventually, as a client grows into additional contract work, management and technical personnel recruiting assistance will probably be called for. At some point in a client's growth, a formal strategic planning process should be developed to make sure that branching out into more complex and higher volume contracts matches the client's long-range objectives.

QUALIFICATIONS AND ORGANIZATION

Competence in government contracting consulting can only come from experience. Getting background information from books or articles won't do the trick. Neither will attending seminars and conferences or classroom study. There is no quick way to gain expertise in this specialty, which is precisely why so little competition exists.

Many consulting firms have seen the benefit of bidding consulting jobs directly with the government. And many of these engagements are extremely lucrative. But very few consulting firms other than engineering, architectural, or design specialists have seen fit to direct their marketing efforts to companies engaged in government contract work.

The best qualifications are derived from previous contract experience. It may have come through employment for a defense contractor or for a government procurement agency. Experience while serving in the armed forces as procurement officer or in other ordnance activities can be invaluable. Short of actual experience in government contracting, you could form a partnership with a more experienced consultant. Once involved in contract work it doesn't take long to pick up the essentials.

Belonging to a consortium with one or more members who are expert in contract work also brings the necessary qualifications to the table, although this is not as effective as having the experience yourself. In the beginning days of my government contracting work

I continually called upon two consortium members to get me through the rough spots.

The first couple of engagements were for small clients bidding contracts of less than $25,000 and I was able to learn on the job. This can be a dangerous practice, however. Clients don't like to pay for non-expert advice. Fortunately, I was able to marry other consulting work with the government contract side during the learning period so clients were not short-changed.

Most management consultants find that expanding the firm to two or more partners before getting into government contracting leads to more spectacular results than would a solo performance. Larger engagements actually require two or more consultants on the job to get it done properly.

As a minimum, partners can be called upon for negotiating, competitive research, and systems assistance. As with other consulting niches, time away from the office can be a killer. With government contracting it's difficult to judge how long an engagement will take, or if it will ever end. It just is not a very good niche market for sole practitioners.

Another way to gain experience is by sub-contracting work from larger consulting firms already involved in government contracts. By learning one piece at a time, such as designing and implementing a cost system or assisting in the development of a quality control system, you eventually build expertise. Government contract engagements with larger clients nearly always require an extra pair of hands. If you let other firms in your area know that you are available when needed, chances are high that sub-contract work will come along.

FEE STRUCTURES AND SCOPE CONTRACT

Because of the wide variety of work in government contracting engagements it's difficult to generalize about fee structures. There really isn't any pat answer. Most firms usually start with hourly billings at about one and one-half times the normal rates for comparable work with non-contracting clients. The larger the client and the greater the size of the contract, the higher the multiple.

From there on, however, creative billing schemes run rampant. The longer the engagement lasts the greater the temptation to bill a flat monthly fee, payable in advance, and based on the estimated days you plan to be on the job that month. Clients that land progress payment contracts will want to tie your payment to their receipt of government payments. High material content contracts bring in large progress payments early in the contract and virtually nothing toward the end. Some consultants negotiate a large retainer out of these early payments and then draw down on it as they go.

One feature of government contract work can throw a clinker into setting an appropriate fee structure. Consulting fees are viewed by the government in the same light as public accounting or legal fees, that is they are considered an administrative expense of the contractor, normally not directly chargeable to a contract. This casts a major shadow over how much progress payments can, or should, be used to pay consultants.

As an administrative expense, not directly chargeable to products, consulting fees must be allocated. To the extent that the contract covers deliveries over several years but the consulting engagement ends near the beginning of the contract, clients often try to pay the fees over the life of the contract rather than when billed. The only feasible way around this problem is to build definitive payment dates into your scope agreement.

Scope agreements must be carefully structured to assure compliance with government contracting regulations, to ensure that consulting fees will be paid on schedule, and to limit your liability. Provisions in many RFPs preclude the use of consultants specifically to assist the client win a contract award. Consequently, scope agreement clauses must clearly define consulting assignments as relating to the total company's operation, not a specific contract.

Specific projects such as designing and implementing cost accounting and quality control systems can be defined. Help in preparing and submitting bid packages can be camouflaged as management assistance in the controllership or marketing areas. Coordination with DCAA auditors and DCAS inspectors falls under the heading of general management counseling. And so on.

Care must also be taken to avoid tying fee payments to receipt of progress payments. General statements referring to payment ten days after receipt of invoice solve this problem. As the engagement progresses and the client begins producing against the contract informal modifications can be negotiated.

Performance liability is normally not a major hurdle in government contract work, although under certain circumstances it can become a nightmare. One of the consultants in our consortium was engaged to assist a client modify an existing cost accounting system to conform to government standards. It passed the preaward survey. As the client began producing against a three year delivery schedule, first line supervisors aborted several of the system's control points in an effort to meet scheduled deliveries.

A DCAA progress audit at the end of the first year (after three-fourths of the total contract value had been collected) resulted in a government claim for one-half of the payments to date ($2.3 million), citing the client's failure to comply with the cost system included in the original RFP. The client turned around and sued the consultant who had designed and assisted in the implementation of the system, claiming negligent performance. The consultant finally won the case, but it took eighteen months of wasted time and legal fees.

Because of the unquestioned authority granted federal procurement and audit agencies, any consulting work is subject to later deficiency charges by the client. Although suits have not yet become a prominent feature in this niche market, as more small contractors enter the field and require an increasing amount of assistance, the number could rise in the future.

Hold harmless provisions should be incorporated in every scope agreement. They don't always hold up but something is better than nothing. Also, liability insurance premiums will be less for engagements that include hold harmless clauses.

MARKETING

An effective marketing campaign includes a two-pronged attack: (1) aim selling efforts directly at potential or existing contractor companies; and, (2) place your consulting qualifications in the hands of appropriate federal procurement offices. Don't expect any direct referrals from these agencies. As previously described, many if not most RFPs preclude prospective contractors from hiring consultants specifically to assist in soliciting, negotiating, or performing against a contract.

Government contracting is a close knit community, however. You keep running into the same DCAS people and procurement officers over and over again. When they know your firm, it doesn't take long for word to spread in private contracting circles that you have the ability and qualifications to do the work. Because so little competition exists in this niche market, prospective clients should soon be pounding at your door.

Rather than contacting procurement agency headquarters offices, you can make much better connections through local offices in your geographic area. Some of the better ones to get to know at this level are:

- General Services Administration (GSA) which purchases "housekeeping" supplies to keep the government running, such as tools, furniture, twine, metalworking equipment, sealers, janitorial supplies, and so on

- Defense Logistics Agency (DLA) which is responsible for buying items for the administrative support of the Department of Defense. DLA is organized into six procurement branches: Defense Construction Supply Center, Defense Fuel Supply Center, Defense Industrial Supply Center, Defense General Supply Center, Defense Electronics Supply Center, and Defense Personnel Support Center.

- The Army Corps of Engineers which purchases goods and services for government architectural, construction, and remodeling projects

- The thirteen federal departments—Agriculture, Commerce, Defense, etc., and the Veteran's Administration (VA). The VA purchases many of the same supplies and equipment directly from contractors that other agencies buy from central supply agencies.

- U.S. Postal Service buys services, vehicles, parts, equipment, and real estate directly from contractors.

- Environmental Protection Agency

- Government Printing Office

- National Aeronautics and Space Administration
- Nuclear Regulatory Commission
- Small Business Administration

Another effective marketing ploy is to select prime and sub-contractors from the *Commerce Business Daily* and make direct calls. All transactions affecting contract bids are listed in the tabloid and at least a percentage of cold calls could bring results.

A more indirect but probably the most effective way of getting government contracting clients is through your existing client base. Many smaller businesses never think of the government as a viable customer. Even when the thought occurs, they shy away because of lack of experience. Once in the door for a project or general management engagement it might make sense to suggest government contracting as a viable expansion tactic. And, quite naturally, you could lead client personnel through the maze of government paperwork and regulations.

Referrals can also be a valuable source of new clients. In the government contracting specialty, however, lawyers, public accountants, and bankers seldom provide much help. The best referrals come from other consultants. Whether part of your consortium or competing in other niches, consulting firms that have clients interested in government contracting but do not have the expertise to handle the engagement are usually willing to let you come in for that specific purpose.

We all know, however, how competing firms guard their clients like a watchdog. The last thing they want is to let another firm in the door to steal future work. Nevertheless, smart consultants realize that to keep clients they must be served. If a client needs government contract expertise it's better to sub-contract the work than lose the client. A very restrictive scope contract will probably have to be executed, but that's to be expected.

Government contracting work is certainly not for everyone. Consulting qualifications can only be achieved through experience. The work can be tedious at times. A great deal of diplomacy is necessary to deal with obstinate and often belligerent government personnel. The risk of performance liability suits runs higher than in other markets. And this is not a good niche for sole practitioners.

On the other hand, very little competition exists. Fees tend to be higher than for other types of engagements. Repeat business is practically assured. And the market will be expanding geometrically for years to come.

Consulting to government contracting clients continues to be one of the few markets within which the actual work performed seems to remain relatively constant over the years. Continual updating of skills and technical capability is not required. And once you learn the ropes, you can rest assured that consulting jobs will continue to flood the gates for as long as you want to stay in the field.

12 The Future of Consulting in a Changing World

Of all the businesses in an ever-changing world, management consulting stands to lose the most by ignoring these shifts. Mind-boggling technological changes, exploding Third World markets, unheard-of creative financing schemes, monopolistic control of world resources, and revolutionary changes in social values will inevitably force companies of every size and shape to adopt new methods for survival. Consulting firms that recognize these radical changes and take steps to adapt their organizations and skills will be the winners. Those intent on looking back will assuredly be out of business in short order.

Long-time consultants who continue to bemoan the loss of clients and the diminishing demand for their antiquated services leave the door wide open for new entrants. As fee scales continue to rise, ex-executives with up-to-date skills will be attracted in ever-increasing numbers. As demands for new problem-solving techniques intensify, college graduates possessing new methodologies will push aside tradition-bound consultants. And as foreign consulting firms wake up to the dearth of competition emanating from our shores, they will capture large and small clients alike from our doorstep.

Developments in the global arena, as well as those closer to home, make it obvious that the business community is undergoing revolutionary changes that prevent a return to the more comfortable, laissez faire environment we have grown accustomed to.

Dreams of truly free markets have been shattered by intensified government controls over our lives and businesses.

Global competition for markets, labor, materials, and money has forced companies to reach out for new ways to stay alive.

Disintegration of the bipolar standoff between the United States and the Soviet Union has left political vacuums throughout the world.

And the hammerlock control of world energy sources forebodes unimagined compromises between both public and private institutions.

Clearly, we have only begun to understand the changing face of our client bases and the demands that current and prospective clients will place on us.

CHANGES IN THE CONSULTING BUSINESS

In the same vein, it's hard to refute that the consulting business itself is undergoing enormous changes. We have already seen the disintegration of tradition bound mid-size consulting firms, as pointed out in Chapter 1. Giants of the industry are clamoring for new approaches to deal with plunging fee income, searching for solutions by acquiring specialized firms with technological expertise they hope will stem the tide. Smaller firms and sole practitioners that have tied their future to fading specialties have either gone out of business or merged with rich big brothers.

Notwithstanding the evolution of the consulting business over the past four years, many additional changes can be expected in the future. Some of the more obvious seem to be:

1. State and federal licensing
2. Growth of multipartner, multinational firms
3. Increase in consulting sub-contract work, moving in all directions between larger firms, smaller firms, and sole practitioners
4. Escalating fees
5. Shifts from hourly billings to flat rates and percentage fees
6. Technical training schools specifically for consultants
7. Graduate work leading to consulting degrees and certification

Licensing and Certification

Consulting is one of the last bastions of pseudo-professional businesses without licensing or certification requirements. Powerful lobbies such as the real estate brokers in California are already pushing licensing legislation.

Self-policing has never worked in the consulting industry. Fiercely independent, most sole practitioners (who make up the bulk of management consultants) refuse to spend valuable time and money belonging to so-called professional consulting organizations for social purposes. Without performance standards or certification requirements they have no incentive to support these clubby groups. And without some type of national organization, industry-wide standards appear impractical.

Nevertheless, under pressure from powerful state and federal self-interest lobbies and fierce competition from foreign firms, many of whom are licensed, it seems likely that our days of freedom are numbered. That being the case it behooves us to take the requisite steps to brush up on our skills to be ready for government, and perhaps industry, controls.

Organizational Changes

The nature of consulting organizational structures is also changing. Demands for technical expertise in a variety of new technologies and the onslaught of foreign ownership of our clients point to increasingly complex, multipartner, and multinational consulting organizations. Now is the time to begin forming such alliances to get in on the ground floor.

Sole practitioners will probably always exist in the consulting business. There will always be those among us who refuse to allow organizational structures to inhibit our freedom. There will always be multipartner firms without the required mix of skills to match client demands who will look to sole practitioner specialists for assistance.

Loose associations such as consortiums and networks offer a partial solution. But farming out work to consortium and network members always diminishes the control you have over the standard of performance and client relationships. The complexities of cross-border client ownership and global operating locations for even the smaller companies demand that we assume control of the work done for our own clients.

Sub-contracting will probably be the wave of the future. Larger firms can sub-contract to sole practitioners for specific tasks without losing control of the engagement. Sole practitioners can sub-contract to larger firms for their specialties and still maintain client loyalty.

New Approaches to Fee Structures

The entire subject of consulting fees is already undergoing revolutionary changes. Trying to keep up with skyrocketing legal and public accounting rates, larger consulting firms have jacked their fees to two to three times what they charged three years ago. Since those firms who have chosen the right market niches are doubling and tripling their billings practically overnight, one must assume that clients are willing to pay these higher fees. That being the case, it seems likely that firms of all sizes will very quickly jump on the bandwagon.

Increasing fees do not always come from higher hourly rates, however. The wave of the future dictates more creativity in establishing our prices. As more and more clients demand implementation assistance rather than merely advice, engagements will become longer and longer. Extended engagements nearly always carry assignments above and beyond the original scope contract.

Clients are no longer satisfied with a quote of hourly rates. They want to know in advance how much the entire job will cost them. The combination of extended engagements and client pressure for firm prices indicates a shift away from hourly rates, to flat fees for the job or percentage fees contingent on accomplishment. Over the next decade the hourly fee will go the way of hourly rates from lawyers, physicians, and public accountants.

Consulting Training

The final major shift in the consulting business will occur in the methodology of learning new skills. Up until now, we have been left to our own devices to scrape out whatever information we could about new techniques and skills to penetrate new market niches. Some of us have carved out niches with on-the-job training through sub-contract work. Others have spent thousands of dollars and untold hours reading and attending seminars and conferences trying to upgrade skills. College graduates enter the business with no practical training at all.

This will change in the not-too-distant future. As licensing and performance standards begin to be felt nationwide, entrepreneurs will quickly see the need for a formal consulting training program. Technical schools will be opened specifically to teach consultants new tricks of the trade. Eventually, graduation from these schools will be a prerequisite for certification, which in turn precedes licensing.

Recognizing the trend, colleges and universities will begin offering consulting curriculum leading to degrees in management consulting. Several schools, such as the Wharton School at the University of Pennsylvania, are already experimenting with similar concepts.

Along with these changes in the consulting industry, massive upheavals are inevitable in nearly every industry from which we draw our clients. The macroeconomic changes described in Chapter 1 signal the demise of traditional consulting markets and orthodox consulting disciplines while opening doors to the thriving market niches described in this book. In addition, several trends have begun to develop that will reinforce the demand for new services and expertise.

CHANGES IN THE LEVEL OF BUSINESS COMPLEXITY

The complexity of conducting even the most straightforward business activity continues to escalate uncontrollably. Municipal, state, and federal government interference in free markets; cross-border alliances and business acquisitions resulting in intensified market competition; an inferior education system resulting in unqualified workers and managers; selling into foreign markets and sourcing foreign capital; acquiring material and labor on global fronts; added responsibilities for social programs: all have combined to make business management more complex than ever before. And the level of complexity is accelerating.

Management rules once thought sacrosanct by such esteemed institutions as the Harvard Business School no longer hold water. The entire economic paradigm of free market trading has fallen by the wayside.

Financial markets, once the domain of corporate issuers and private investors, are now controlled by foreign governments and financial institutions, overlaid with inhibiting federal regulations. Theories that relate labor productivity to corporate earnings and management incentives to improved performance are as antiquated as the textbooks they come from. Political power groups once thought to be the province of corporate giants have transcended into the realm of environmentalists, minority activists, social welfare supporters, and even foreign government lobbyists.

World tensions will exacerbate well into the 21st century. New power struggles over control of the world's oil supply will ignite further wars and civil uprisings. Economic assistance from Europe and the United States to the Soviet Union, African nations, South Asia, and Latin America will drain resources away from the development of alternate energy sources. The world's continued dependence on oil will focus economic and political attention on the Middle East and a permanent resolution of Israeli-Arab differences.

The destructiveness of these efforts will lead to the opening of enormous markets for military hardware and support materiel, food products, medical supplies, and eventually massive infrastructure rebuilding. Global financial resources that would otherwise be funneled to industrialized nations will focus on building the economic and military might of Middle East antagonists.

Companies with a global mindset will see the opening and augment their traditional markets with products and services to fill these needs. Consulting firms that have made the effort to become international in scope will be in the forefront to assist clients in every phase of expansion into Middle East and other global markets.

Management Techniques

With the disappearance of traditional management techniques and historical business forces, an enormous vacuum in management philosophy and control has occurred. No single force or group has stepped forward to point the way out of this abyss of confusion. Business leaders and political pundits struggle for an answer while small and mid-size companies flounder in deep water, waiting and hoping for solutions.

The consulting industry offers a bridge to the future. As independent advisors skilled in new management techniques and abreast of technological developments, consultants can focus management attention on new strategic solutions to operating problems.

Accessibility to data banks of global information is enabling consultants to steer clients through competitive underbrush and assist them in developing new products and services to meet new market demands. With direct ties to professional sources of financing, legal, and tax advice, consultants can direct clients to a cacophony of resources that would be otherwise unavailable. As intermediaries without a proprietary interest in a client's affairs, consultants can interface with regulatory bodies, government officials, foreign intermediaries, and potential joint venture partners to open doors to new projects and customers.

Consultants who are willing and able to remain on the leading edge of global technology, resources, and markets will fill the vacuum for clients between what was and what is to come. As this leading edge keeps moving outward, consultants should continue to set the pace in the development of new management techniques to match customer demand. At the same time those well-versed in the globalization of ownership and control can assist clients build on these new relationships.

Redirected Company Missions

Shifting customer priorities stimulated by redirected social values create a new role for the consulting industry. Where government regulations have failed to stem the tide of environmental destruction, socially conscious customers will have a pronounced effect. Consumer pressure has already forced companies to change their practices in the tuna industry, the Brazilian rain forests, ocean dumping, offshore oilwell drilling, lumbering in the Northwest, and hazardous waste disposal. Solid waste recycling facilities springing up across the country reflect a response to consumer pressure, as do the massive changes in the packaging industry.

These changes are a small fraction of what can be expected in the future. As described in Chapter 5, consulting firms specializing in environmental protection markets stand to clean up not only during the next decade but well into the 21st century. Firms with international experience can also take advantage of environmental projects around the world, such as the recent oil spill cleanup and oilwell reconstruction following the Persian Gulf debacle. Many other socially conscious moves are afoot both in America and abroad. Corporate social responsibility will become the byword for future success in the global economy.

If they choose, consultants can be at the forefront of assisting companies to introduce products and services to stem the tide of famine and pestilence in Africa and South Asia. They can provide management leadership to coordinate urban redevelopment projects for housing, health care, schools, and recreation facilities in disadvantaged neighborhoods of our inner cities. With the proper sourcing techniques, consultants can intercede between government and private industry to form joint ventures for life support research projects.

Strategic Planning

This shift in corporate values from short-term gains to long-range social responsibility creates a whole new ballgame in strategic planning disciplines. Market definitions, research and development programs, customer service facilities, and marketing tactics must be adjusted to reflect the achievement of long-term social goals as well as company profitability and market control.

New pricing techniques demanded by socially and economically deprived consumer groups both in this country and abroad will force a reassessment of manufacturing processes. Lower prices and higher quality products will force the introduction of heretofore unknown materials into product design and engineering applications.

Consulting firms will be called upon to assist, and in some instances for smaller companies, direct this strategic planning process. Engineering design skills will be matched with new market and product analysis techniques. Consultants with a global view will be able to help clients structure their strategic plans to incorporate social market demands from around the world.

Personnel Selection and Training

The shift to socially responsive strategies and tactics will require a new breed of management personnel, managers who look at a company's achievements in the social arena as paramount for long-term growth and stability. Consulting firms that maintain a data base of multinational executives will have the inner track with clients to assist in recruiting and/or training appropriate, socially conscious managers.

Radical changes in employee values and expectations will follow the shift to social responsibility. Organizational structures must reflect these changes. As independent observers imbued with methods for making these adjustments, consultants will become intimately involved in restructuring organizational lines of authority and responsibility.

Employee Motivation Techniques

Consultants can also lead the way in the introduction of new motivational tools. Work place "community" concepts will become the standard procedure in most companies. "Community" will serve as the primary structure for motivating employees as well as rewarding them. Practicing the principles of community in a work environment allows individuals to "communicate with authenticity, deal with difficult issues, bridge differences with integrity, and relate one to another with love and respect." (From the mission statement of the Foundation for Community Encouragement.) In a nutshell, structuring a company's organization along "community" lines encourages the same social consciousness to be practiced within the organization as the company holds out to the public through its advertising, product introductions, and customer service activities.

To participate in the revolution of employee relationships, consultants must undergo an intensive learning process, picking up skills in group dynamics and social psychology necessary to implement "community" principles. Intuitively, many will disagree with the effectiveness of these principles in the work place. The development of "community" tools is still in the embryonic stage.

Nevertheless, several smaller consulting firms serving national markets are already deeply involved in learning and teaching these skills. Regardless of current skepticism, consulting firms of the future must be in a position to explain and implement "community" concepts if they expect to compete for engagements in any phase of organization development.

Within this macro setting, radical micro changes will also occur. The most dynamic changes will be in the cost structures of businesses and products, the internal systems to accumulate and measure these costs, and the very structure of the business itself.

THE CHANGING STRUCTURE OF BUSINESS

The intensification of complexities will create radical changes in the cost of doing business. Drawing from the supercomputer technology of today, the next generation of business computers will radically alter the way businesses are organized, how companies interface with customers and suppliers, and the rapid deployment of goods and services. There will be a revolution in the entire manufacturing process.

Far fewer personnel will be needed to produce and sell goods and services. Middle managers as we use the term today will become outmoded, replaced by instant communication technology, computer based performance measures and expense controls, zero defect production machinery, and computer selling and ordering technology. Emphasis will be placed on highly skilled specialists on factory floors, "star wars" transport of goods and people, and computer designed products. Top executives will focus on maintaining public profiles and complying with government mandates.

The inflexibility of operating costs under this scenario will be staggering. As the number of employees decreases and computer controlled robotics handle all but the most sophisticated operating functions, companies will be unable to cut costs during downturns merely be laying off people. There won't be enough people on the payroll to make a difference.

Instead, companies must look to better methods for selecting and controlling product and customer mix. They must concentrate on ever-more efficient matching of market demand and production capability. And most important, they must look to guidance and direction from outside the company for creative ways to minimize costs and increase sales, which of course is where management consultants come in.

This dramatic change in cost structures will force even recalcitrant executives to source materials, labor, and money worldwide. Some of these resources will be available in the free-market: most will be controlled by government bodies.

Government Control

As the gap between the "haves" and the "have nots" expands geometrically, demands for a reallocation of the world's resources will force governments into an active role in controlling public and private access to financial resources. It will also force governments into alliances aimed at controlling the global distribution of food, shelter, medical care, communications, and transportation.

Agriculture will come increasingly under government supervision to control prices and distribution to the needy. Socialized medicine will prevail throughout the world to ensure adequate health care for the poor and the elderly. Central to national and regional security and paramount for the equitable distribution of goods and services, both the communications and transportation industries will fall under worldwide government control. Inefficient sovereign states will band together to create monopolistic cartels restricting access to the world's natural resources, from lumber to oil, from magnesium to coal, from fresh water to sea life.

Accelerating U.S. and foreign government controls foretell three massive changes in the way business will be conducted:

- Government services will attract thousands of experienced, middle manager executives with power positions and super compensation packages.

- Companies will have to deal with foreign government officials as well as with those in the United States.

- Thousands of executives and middle managers will opt for entrepreneurship as opposed to government positions or lessened responsibilities in corporations.

Changes In the Composition of Companies

A second, and probably more serious, fallout of technologically created high costs of doing business and escalating government interference in global market economies will be a radical change in the composition of companies. The Fortune 100 will inevitably grow even larger and stronger. With roots firmly established on foreign soil to corral global resources and active roles in influencing and even setting government policies, these giants can only expand their influence in the market place.

The Fortune 100 of American companies will evolve into the Fortune 100 of global companies as giant global mergers bring competitors together under one roof. As giants grow to supergiants, their willingness to take risks will decreases.

New product introductions funded by government grants, the exploration for new markets, the development of creative management techniques, and a host of other risk-oriented ventures will increasingly become the domain of smaller companies using entrepreneurial approaches to problem solving. Small businesses will always play a critical role in the world business scene.

Between the supergiants and small businesses, currently defined mid-size companies will find little sustenance in the leftovers. Most will fold. Those struggling to remain must either join forces with the supergiants or have the deep pockets to carve out new market niches. The latter case will inevitably result in restructuring balance sheets and product lines and ultimately downsizing to join the ranks of small business.

The demise of mid-size companies will occur gradually over several years, hardly noticeable in the competitive landscape. Many industries have witnessed the beginning of this trend already. The publishing, hospitality, semiconductor, communications (telephone and television broadcasting especially), and newspaper industries have already succumbed to economies of scale.

Traditionally, principles of economies of scale related only to the upward consolidation of activities in larger corporations capable of achieving lower unit costs by eliminating redundant personnel and operations and by purchasing materials and facilities in bulk. In the future the term will also apply to small companies, reducing unit costs by personnel efficiency, low overhead, and flexibility.

Impact on Management Consulting

Advances in automated technology, accelerated government controls, and shifts in the size and composition of companies will have a major impact on the future of management consulting. Demand will come from four sources:

1. Government agencies. The explosion in the number of management people in government positions, in the United States as well as foreign governments, will create a chaotic mix of professional bureaucrats accustomed to slow, lumbering, paper filled procedures and professional business managers demanding rapid responses, quick decisions, and the flexibility to achieve results.

Gridlock can only be avoided by introducing independent consultants well-versed in modern management techniques and capable of interfacing with both parties to reach resolution on new operating procedures. The definition of workable organization responsibilities, the introduction of meaningful strategic planning processes, the recruiting of management personnel, financial forecasting, and many other activities will be spearheaded by consultants.

2. Corporate supergiants. Although these behemoths will have sufficient expertise to handle mergers, new financing, and other internal matters, the new relationships with government bodies around the world will cause bureaucratic holdups and proprietary disagreements. Management consultants will be able to provide a valuable linking interface between U.S. and foreign government agencies and the supergiants. Consultants will also assist in filling the vast organizational gaps left by middle managers departing for government service and entrepreneurship.

3. Small businesses. The rapid growth of small businesses using high tech administrative and production equipment will accelerate the same group of operating problems present in today's environment, with one difference. With access to high technology, the complexity of the solutions to these problems will increase geometrically.

In addition to assisting entrepreneurs resolve their normal operating problems, consultants will be a major force in introducing small businesses to global trade, without which they will not be able to survive. As government control grows, the complexity of compliance reporting will escalate and the need for assistance in this area will be more pronounced than it is today. Finally, consultants will act in the same liaison function with government bureaucrats as they will for the supergiants.

4. Mid-size companies. Caught in the restructuring squeeze, mid-size companies will need consultants more than any other group. Mid-size companies provide the largest group of prospective clients needing help in downsizing their operations. They will need assistance in adjusting the organizations, systems, planning, financing, market and customer selection, and product line modification to reflect lower operating levels.

This will become an extremely lucrative niche because very little competition exists, or is likely to exist. For the same reasons that consultants stay away from troubled company consulting described in Chapter 10, most avoid downsizing engagements. In addition, very few consultants have the background and skills to offer meaningful downsizing services.

As structural changes occur en masse, additional consultants will inevitably be attracted to these market niches. However, with the rapid increase in the number of companies needing consulting services there should be plenty of room for everyone.

THE CHANGING FINANCIAL SYSTEM

The banking system as we have known it for generations is beginning to disintegrate. Inevitably, banking regulations will be rewritten to allow banks entry into non-bank activities and permit private companies to own banks. This mixing of provider and user of funds will signal the end of all but a few multinational banks as providers of public growth capital. Banks will continue to function as depositories and clearing houses but lending and other business support activities will be restricted to a bank's private interests. The demise of the traditional banking system opens the door to more creative lending and investing opportunities from new sources of capital.

The major sources of new capital will emanate from global investors and central governments. The increasing concentration of wealth, both legally and illegally gained, in the hands of a limited number of individuals and countries foretells revolutionary changes in the way individuals, companies, and nations will finance their activities.

Escalating operating costs will force companies to scan the global horizon for new funding. Since money knows no national boundaries, lenders and investors from Asia to the Middle East will place their funds where they can expect the highest returns and the greatest safety.

Governments will also get into the act. Increasing government control and ownership of private industry places the burden of business growth squarely on the shoulders of public leaders and government agencies. Central banks will become major financiers of private industry. Cross-border company ownership will create cross-border financing from government sources as well as from private financial institutions and investors.

The supergiants, and especially those controlling the energy (read oil), communications, and transportation industries, will be in the forefront of shaping financial instruments and procedures to manage true private and governmental cross-border financing. They will set the financial market ground rules for private lenders and investors as well as governments.

In both the private and public sectors of the domestic economy these changes are already visible. Using Treasury borrowings (which ultimately means taxpayer dollars), the federal government has pumped massive amounts of new capital into companies in the hospitality, alternate energy research, medical and pharmaceutical, banking, aerospace, and commercial and industrial real estate development industries.

In the private sector, new non-bank banks owned and financed by multinational freight forwarding companies (e.g., LEP PLC from Great Britain), states (e.g., the California Export Finance Office), cities (e.g., LAXport from Los Angeles), and industrial supergiants (e.g., General Electric) have developed creative new methods for funding specific transactions as well as entire operations.

Smaller operating companies and entrepreneurial start-ups, together with mid-size companies that remain competitive, will be faced with challenges for raising capital along unfamiliar avenues. Most will be required to give up equity shares for both short and long-term funding. This in turn will exacerbate the already accelerating complexity of company ownership and control.

The proliferation of federal, state, and municipal funding sources; foreign government lending and investing schemes, and private global lending and investing sources; the internationalization of major world stock exchanges; the increasing importance of countertrade agreements (domestically and overseas): all present qualified management consultants with unequaled opportunities. Consultants will become a necessary link between these complex financing sources and smaller operating companies.

Most of these companies will remain unsophisticated in the world financial system. They will need assistance in sourcing, structuring, and negotiating new capital requirements. In addition, many will look to consultants to assist in refinancing existing burdensome debt with these new capital sources.

To take advantage of the burgeoning demand for financing assistance, consultants will have to become knowledgeable in a variety of new financing forms and methods. They will need to become adept at weighing a client's advantages and risks from alternative sources. Many new financing arrangements will require equity sharing, joint ventures with unknown partners, integration of market and customer selection with financing availability (including selling directly to or utilizing the financing source), and in many cases, after-sale countertrade and customer service activities totally dependent on the source and structure of financing.

Furthermore, five broad prerequisites will be mandatory to provide effective consulting advice in the new financial markets. Consulting firms should:

1. Be well-versed in the methods and forms of international trade. It will no longer be possible to grow a consulting business without becoming globally involved.

2. Structure internal organizations that can handle diverse, integrated global and domestic assignments from the same client. This will require creative forms of partnerships and joint venture arrangements to ensure consulting qualifications in diverse disciplines.

3. Develop a repertoire of domestic political connections at the federal, state, and municipal levels that can be called upon to open appropriate financial doors.
4. Consciously build up a cadre of professional and bureaucratic connections in major global trading areas for assistance in sourcing and structuring financing options.
5. Build a data base by country and/or region of information necessary to provide prompt, efficient service to clients. Included should be data pertaining to financing sources, alternate structuring requirements, special barriers and incentives, names and addresses of government and professional contacts, licensing and permit regulations, and labor and material resource availability.

PLANNING FOR THE FUTURE

There can be little doubt that the management consulting industry of the future will look entirely different from that of the present. Just as with industrial and commercial industries, large consulting firms will become superpowers, smaller firms will find blossoming new markets, and mid-size firms will adjust either by merging into large firms or downsizing.

The accelerating complexity of the business environment and business structures prohibits consultants from burying their heads in the sand, pretending that domestic business is still confined within the borders of the United States and that international business is a unique, often incomprehensible specialty. We must become globally oriented for the same reason our clients must look beyond their immediate markets. We must be willing to develop our resources and skills on a global plane. We must adopt a true global mindset.

As the next decade turns into the 21st century those of us unwilling or unable to recognize the shift to a world economy and a multinational business community will be crying the same blues so many "professional" consultants proclaim today—that the demand for consultants is dropping dramatically, and that the consulting business is a mature industry, sliding down the slippery slope to oblivion.

As we advise our clients to plan ahead, so must we. Ignoring the benefits of a well thought out strategic plan for our own businesses seems to be a sure road to disaster. Coping with new client demands of the future will take more than wishful thinking. It will certainly take a different approach from that espoused by my Baltimore friend "The whole trick in successful marketing is to identify what the client needs and then get out and sell it to him."

Just as with strategic planning engagements, the starting point of our own plans should be a clear definition of our objectives, both personal and for the firm. If we don't know where we want to be we certainly can't figure out how to get there. Do we plan to remain in consulting or is this merely a stepping stone to another career objective? Can we work with partners or must we traverse the road alone? Do family and other personal commitments allow enough flexibility to meet our objectives or must one or the other give ground? We all know what questions to ask ourselves: the same ones we tell clients to ask.

Obviously, we must decide the specific market niches we wish to go after to meet our objectives. Perhaps it's a two or three stage approach, building new markets on what we already have? Or perhaps we should phase out of a current client base that prohibits expansion and flexibility? Regardless of which markets make the most sense from a strategic perspective, the rapidly changing business climate demands that all management consultants who expect to be around ten years from now adopt or broaden three strategic principles:

1. Global mindset. Except for neighborhood "ma and pa" businesses, companies of all sizes and in virtually any industry must look to global sources for financing and materials. Many will opt to market directly or indirectly to foreign customers. Many more will enter into sub-contract agreements with supergiants or government agencies. Regardless of the path, nearly all clients of the future will be involved in international trade of one type or another.

To get and keep these clients, consultants must look at all businesses through global glasses. We must take off the blinders and acknowledge that global trade is here to stay and client problems will require global solutions.

2. Financial acumen. The days of "the customer is king" will rapidly fade from sight. Money will become the cornerstone of future business, the most important company asset, the primary building block for growth. Customers will increasingly demand financial assistance from sellers. Companies must be in a position to provide capital not only for their internal growth but on a transactional basis for their customers. This capital will be multinational, with no one country or region in control.

Consultants can no longer turn a blind side to the symbiotic relationship of finance, market, and ultimately personnel effectiveness. We must base our advice for the solution of internal client problems, for strategic plans, and for market/product evaluations not only on operational considerations, but more important, on financing availability and form. We must become expert in dealing with global financial markets to efficiently counsel our clients for virtually any major engagement.

3. Connections. With government bureaucrats, foreign owners and financiers, multinational resources, and global market shifts, consultants must establish a worldwide data bank of political, professional, and financial contacts. So many future business decisions will be predicated on subtle influences and referrals that it will be impossible to offer workable solutions to clients without such resources at our disposal. The economics of Adam Smith have disappeared in the morass of global dealings. We must get on the bandwagon and recognize the inherent value of political pressure points, or become ineffective as advice givers.

Within this chapter, and in fact throughout this entire book, I have attempted to outline the most likely conditions affecting the successful operation of management consulting businesses over the next decade and into the 21st century. Certainly the market niches, skills, and procedural steps recommended herein are not inclusive. For every idea presented, other long-term consultants can probably come up with five more. The debate over the effectiveness of large versus small consulting firms, or sole practitioners, has raged for decades and will continue unabated, just as the benefits of specializing in large or small clients remain unresolved.

Notwithstanding the obvious omissions and argumentative conclusions, the market niches described in previous chapters have a high likelihood of substantial growth over the next decade. It is also difficult to debate that the business world has recently experienced and will continue to undergo revolutionary changes. And few long-time consultants who read or hear of current events would dispute that the United States and world economies have taken on a strong global flavor.

The main thrust of these ideas and suggestions is to open doors to future opportunities, many of which will involve becoming knowledgeable in the international arena. If nothing else has been accomplished, I hope to have alerted you to the fundamental requirement of adopting a global mindset in order to remain successful in your consulting business during the years ahead. Good hunting.

Index